Beauty expert Oleda Baker says:

"Calendar age is unimportant. What matters is that you develop a taste for life that will keep you interested . . . interesting . . . desirable and sexually active for as young as you live."

Why 29 Forever?

"Because 29 is such an attractive age, both physically and mentally. It's young, but not ingenue young. At 29 you are (hopefully) experienced in the ways of the world and have some notion of who you are and what you want out of life. You're old enough to have learned from your experiences, but you aren't jaded. Never pessimistic. . . . You're sensuous and appealing and buoyantly healthy. . . . You're at your peak!"

The beauty adventure of your life is about to begin. Turn the page and you're one step closer to 29 Forever . . .

29 FOREVER

BY OLEDA BAKER
WITH BILL GALE

A BERKLEY BOOK
published by
BERKLEY PUBLISHING CORPORATION

To my wonderful, high-spirited son, David,
who certainly helps to keep his mom...29 Forever

To my dear sister, Carmen,
who is one of the sweetest persons I know.

And to all *women who seek the 29 Forever spirit.*

Contents

Introduction: Yes, You Can!   ix

1) I Believe...   1

2) Know Thyself... Love Thyself   15

3) The Skin Game   23

4) Drinking and Smoking: The Beauty Killers   47

5) About Face!   53

6) Corrective Makeup   61

7) The Body Beautiful   67

8) Those Fabulous Extremities:
   Feet and Legs   89

9) Hands Up!   99

10) Hair: Nature's Miracle Fiber   105

11) A Luscious, Young Mouth—
    With a Voice to Match   127

12) Beauty Sleep   133

13)	Eat and Grow Younger	141
14)	... With an Assist from Mother Nature	157
15)	How "Scentuous" Can You Get?	161
16)	How Your Sex Life Affects the Way You Look, Feel, And Think	169
17)	The Female Orgasm	173
18)	The Orgasm As a Beautifier—It Will Help You Stay 29 Forever	177
19)	The Psychological Approach to the Beauty-Orgasm	183
20)	Before-Orgasm Beauty Treatments	189
21)	Beauty Benefits During Orgasm	201
22)	How the Proper Vitamins, Minerals, and Nutrition Help You Achieve Beauty-Orgasm	219
23)	Drinking, Smoking, and "the Pill": Beauty-Orgasm Killers	227
24)	The Problem of "Frigidity"	231
25)	The "Complete" Woman	239

INTRODUCTION
Yes, You Can!

Yes, you *can* be 29 Forever.

. . . Provided you believe you can. Wishing won't make it so. But willing it will. Believe it. And you're on your way.

Exactly what *is* the 29 Forever concept? Well, it's more than just your physical appearance—it's also your psychological attitude *and* your spiritual belief. It's the determination to make the most of each day, no matter what your chronological age, lifestyle, or handicaps may be. It does not allow you to make excuses for not doing the things you are supposed to be doing. It's a POSITIVE THINKING PROCESS!

After all, who controls your life? *You* do. You can change your life. No one or nothing can stop you. So don't put off living life to the hilt another minute.

Think Big. Start Small. Take your first step now (and you have . . . you picked up this book), and it will lead to another step . . . and then another bigger, even more adventurous step. You'll begin to feel better and better about YOU, and soon people will start reacting positively to that. Doors that were closed to you—or only half-ajar—will open wide. I know, because today, at forty-two, I'm far younger, healthier, happier than I ever was at twenty or thirty.

But don't take my word for it. Test it for yourself. Can you spare thirty seconds? "Of course!" you say, but what can you do in just thirty seconds? *Plenty.*

Tomorrow morning, before you really start your day, spend thirty seconds to tidy your hair . . . and dab a little cream rouge on your cheeks for a glow. With the smidgin left on your fingertip, smooth it across your lips. Presto! You will look and feel *special.* It will work like a little bouquet of flowers . . . or a whispered compliment . . . from You to You. I promise you it won't be just another ho-hum morning. It will be the start of a very Good Morning!

Look in the mirror. Smile at the woman you see reflected there. She's your friend. Your best friend. The NEW you. And you're about to construct a whole new life. Step by step. Chapter by chapter.

That's right, chapter by chapter. Because this book is going to show you how. How to become an achiever, a doer. How to become the kind of woman who knows who she is . . . what she wants . . . and how to get it. A woman who is sensuous and is determined to stay that way all her life, because she knows that her sexuality is vital to her happiness as well as her physical, emotional, and mental well-being. And, of course, she's beautiful—inside and outside. *Every* woman is capable of such beauty. I feel sure you go along with the idea that every woman can develop a beautiful inner self; but perhaps you look in your mirror and—possibly from the habit of negative thinking—you seek out your least attractive feature and tell yourself that *you* can never be physically beautiful. Nonsense! Barbra Streisand—the only female motion picture star among today's top ten box office draws—is certainly not a conventional beauty. Neither is Liza Minnelli, or television's super glamour-girl, Cher. But, oh my, the number of women who envy them and their allure!

Now if the thought of looking and feeling beautiful is unsettling, then this book is not for you. But if that thought excites you, then read on. *You* can be 29 Forever. Because if I can . . . you can.

Calendar age is unimportant. What matters is that you develop a taste for life that will keep you interested . . . interesting . . . desirable and sexually active for as long as you live.

"Don't ever say anything to me about age," says one of the happiest, most vital women I know. "I have a very gay nature and I just will not let myself down." And I'm firmly convinced she never will. In the words of *The New York Times*: ". . . her face made up with great care and her hair modishly arranged . . . her head held high . . . she could be a fashion consultant for a highstyle store." Her calendar age? A snappy eighty-nine. But of course she's really 29 . . . Forever.

Just as you are going to be, too. Somewhere

between now and the time you reach the last page, there will be a kind of soundless click. You'll hear it, and feel it. That will be the precise moment it takes hold of you for life. And you will never be the same again. Because from that moment on, dear friend, you will be 29 Forever.

1

I Believe . . .

AT FORTY-TWO, I am beginning one of the most exciting times of my life. I'm writing this, my fourth book, and I have begun a cosmetic business for which I do my own modeling in both the print and television advertising, in which my calendar age and my 29 Forever appearance are quite naturally strong selling points. As a result, people are beginning to recognize me on the street and occasionally I feel a hand on my arm and I turn to find someone who says—eyes scanning my face— "You're not really forty-two, are you?"

Well, I'm not only forty-two, but I'm also happier today than I was at twenty-two. In fact, I'm so passionately involved with TODAY, that when my editor for this book asked that I write something about what I was like years ago, I practically drew a blank. So I contacted my elder sister, Carmen, on her farm in North Carolina and asked her to stop minding the goats and collecting the eggs for a moment, and give some concentrated thought to me. What, I asked, did she remember about me when we were teenagers and still living at home with our parents?

"You were the proverbial ugly duckling," she replied, almost too quickly. "Sickly... a bit hunchback... and not good in school subjects of reading and spelling." Well, I'm no longer sickly or hunchback (contrary to Carmen, I was only slightly round shouldered), and I can read like a whiz. But, for the life of me, I still can't spell.

Anyway, as you can readily see, sister Carmen doesn't mince words.

Next, I contacted my younger sister, Francey, who lives in Fort Worth, Texas... is thirty-three... married with two children... and is an interior designer.

She replied: "You have been a mother image to me for many years. You always tried to understand my problems and did your best to help me solve them. I learned to rely on you for guidance."

Next, my brother, Harry, had this to say: "You were the first to step out and achieve something on your own." Then, after some characteristic hemming and hawing, "I believe from the health angle, you have influenced me to the point I'm aware of my weight and that pretty girls like trim guys."

My mother, Thelma Freeman, who detests writing letters, nevertheless put pen to paper and this is the result: "You were a shy, unselfish child, but you learned not to let anyone push you about when you were still very young."

My father, Marvin Freeman, who is now married

to a delightful woman eight years my junior, wrote
from Florida: "I think you must have inherited your
determination from both your parents. It seems to
me you were always more inquisitive and daring."

Why did I canvass my family with regard to the
fledgling me of twenty or more years ago? Because I
don't trust my own memory of that girl. Because, at
forty-two, I feel and think so much younger than she
did.

Mother and I are the blondes in the family;
Carmen and Francey are the brunettes. Or rather I
should say, mother and I are the blondes by choice;
Carmen and Francey are brunettes by birth. I
colored my hair blonde at age twenty-three. My
natural shade was medium brown. Pleasant, but not
exciting. My husband and my father admired my
new blondeness, but my mother thought I had
ruined myself. Today, mother—in her early
sixties—is a slim and lovely blonde herself. So you
see, I spring from a family dedicated to change and
the challenge of the *new*.

It's the question of how to get your head on
straight and keep it that way—no matter how many
candles are flickering on your birthday cake.

Mother's mother, Emma Miller, is eighty-five
and she often drives the "old" people in her
neighborhood to the store to help them buy their
groceries. She is a substitute teacher in a nursery
school in Ft. Lauderdale, Florida; and while I doubt
that she will ever decide to become a blonde, who
knows? For she, too, is 29 Forever. When that is
your philosophy, there is no room in your
vocabulary for the word IF. If there were, I wouldn't

3

be here in New York at this moment writing this book at age forty-two . . . my chronological age. My true age is 29. Forever!

29 Forever is a daily approach to life. It starts in your head and then fills your entire being until it becomes a way of life. You may be one of those very lucky women who was born with that *no-room-for-IF, anything-is-possible, let-me-at-it* attitude toward the business of living. If you are—my congratulations. Most of us have to cultivate it. But once it becomes part of you, you needn't think about it every day. It's just there, like a dedicated, delightful companion who gives your life color, sparkle, and infinite joy.

I had to cultivate the 29 Forever approach to life. After all, as my sister Carmen reminded me, I was the proverbial ugly duckling. You'll see this for yourself when you look at the photographs of me in this book. Although styles have changed—and everyone's idea of what constitutes beauty—I think you'll agree that, at forty-two, I look better than I ever have. I also *feel* better than I ever have, which is, of course, what being 29 Forever is all about.

Not only was I the ugly duckling, I was also painfully shy. By fourteen, I had attained my full height of 5'8". I was thin, too thin, I thought then. Today when I look at snapshots taken back in those days, I realize that I was really rather fashionably skinny—but I didn't feel fashionable!

At fifteen, I was still so shy that it was practically impossible for me to get up in front of the class for anything, even to sharpen a pencil. By the end of that school year, however, I decided I had to do something positive about ME. And so there it was:

4

the very first glimmer of the 29 Forever spirit poking its way into my consciousness.

So what did I do? I signed up for Dramatics. A perfectly idiotic, blissfully idiotic thing for me to do. But I realized I was growing inward, and that is most certainly not the direction for anyone to go. I was growing old at fifteen, because I considered copping out, which would limit my growth and awareness of life. I had to stop that, shift gears, and go *full speed ahead*. I did it at fifteen. You can do it at fifty-one. Or sixty-one. The main thing is to *do* it.

That summer, thinking about Dramatics in the fall, I was terrified. Still, I wouldn't consider dropping out. I decided I must go through with it. Like the legendary Scarlett O'Hara, I would handle it when the time came.

It came, and I discovered that it was too difficult for me to act onstage. But I still didn't give up and admit defeat! I tried a different direction and found that I could direct plays. In fact, I became such a good director that, at the end of my junior year, I won the Best Director award—which was traditionally awarded only to a senior.

The next year I won it again. So there it was; I had taken my first step toward making the 29 Forever philosophy my own. I had reason to be proud of myself. I was thinking outside myself at last . . . and starting to take an *active* part in life. I began to stop walking round shouldered. I stood tall and proud. I still couldn't spell, but I had discovered I had other talents. But I still didn't think of myself as really attractive.

Now, once you develop the 29 Forever attitude, good things just naturally follow; because your head is on straight, and you're looking forward instead of backward.

Still, what happened in my senior year came as a surprise—no, it came more like a shock. *I was chosen to be a calendar girl.* No, not a nude calendar girl. I wore a blue summer dress with puffed sleeves and I carried a basket of flowers. I was the merry month of May. (No matter that I was born in August.) To be chosen to be one of the twelve calendar girls—out of a graduating class of six hundred—was an honor. Tall, stringy me, when there were so many cutely rounded girls with effervescent personalities and lots of boyfriends.

I also acquired my first admirer at this time—a man of twenty-four. (Since I was taller than most of the boys in my class and thought "boys" were silly, I hadn't made much of an impression on the males in my class.) I wasn't allowed to date, so my new admirer took me to church and, on the way home, bought me ice cream sodas. On our very first "encounter," one of the cutely rounded girls from school, who worked at the soda fountain, took notice and was obviously impressed. The next day, Oleda Freeman—the merry month of May—was suddenly the center of attraction. For the females, that is. Girls who had never done more than nod in my direction were now stopping to chat. They were impressed, which impressed me. My status changed. In the immortal words of sister Carmen: I had become "the rose" and she "a faded daisy." I was now full of the 29 Forever spirit.

I married David Pettis at twenty-one. We both worked for the telephone company in Miami; I had a clerical job and David installed phones. He was pleasant and fun to be with, and in those days, you were expected to marry young and raise a family. To show you just how sensible and circumspect I was at that age, during our engagement we bought a three-bedroom house and started furnishing it. After a huge church wedding (I had five bridesmaids), we moved into our new home. A honeymoon trip would have seemed frivolous.

With my husband's encouragement, I went to modeling school. I became a blonde at twenty-three, and a mother at twenty-four. I went back to modeling after my son, David, was born. The head of the model agency kept after me to go to New York City and try for "the big time." My husband urged me to go, too. He was never jealous of my career.

Then one day we learned that a friend was driving to New York and he offered to take me along. I was twenty-six. Some models are "finished" at twenty-six. What if I failed? Only a fleeting thought. 29 Forever had gotten to me. I rejected the word "IF." Still, I did hesitate. I had a loving husband and an adorable baby. Was I leaving a happy, comfortable home in sunny Florida for a rat race in smog-filled New York? But my husband said GO, and his mother, whom I loved dearly, offered to take care of him and little David. Furthermore, it was agreed that I would fly back to Miami every three weeks. Yet, while we were putting my luggage in the trunk of our friend's car, I had second thoughts. GO or STAY? My husband kissed me goodbye and, after that, the 29 Forever spirit sped me on my way north as much as our friend's car did.

My first full day in New York, I sat down and

dialed two of the top modeling agencies in the city. Both asked me my height. Then each gave me an appointment. At the first interview, I was accepted, so I cancelled the second appointment.

I began the rounds of the advertising agencies and photographers via foot and bus; I had no money for taxis. In fact, I had no money to speak of. When the model agency learned of this, I was advanced $500 against my future earnings. That was a vote of confidence and a boost to my ego. 29 Forever became even more a part of me. So naturally, good things started happening.

Immediately I was sent to Kenneth, the now internationally famous hair stylist, who at that time headed the salon at Lily Daché. Actually, I was sent there for the sole purpose of having that divinely talented man style my hair and get it in shape for modeling assignments. But he liked me and set up a booking (modeling assignment) for me on the spot. My agency was ecstatic. Overnight I was a $40-an-hour model (starting fee then was usually $25) and, within six weeks, I was posing for *Vogue* magazine. Next came those extremely lucrative television commercials. Suddenly, I was in demand.

Earlier than expected I managed to fly home to Miami for a few days. I just couldn't stand being away from my husband and baby any longer. We talked things over and my husband decided to transfer to New York. So, in just seven weeks, we were a family again; this time living in the heart of the Big City. I acquired a sleep-in housekeeper and I worked five days a week...every week. Some mornings, when I had a TV commercial on my schedule, I had to rise at 5:30 A.M. It was not, I grant you, an ideal lifestyle. I had little time to spend with my husband and our relationship began to suffer. Modeling was terribly demanding. Evenings were usually spent preparing for the next day's assignment.

After two years in New York, David and I agreed to separate. No hard feelings. New York was simply not his town; it had become mine. He returned to Miami and I remained in New York with our little son. Not long afterward, we divorced.

I now threw myself into my modeling career completely. For the first time in my life, I didn't have someone to lean on, having gone from my parents' home into marriage. Now, alone in New York City, I was determined to prove to myself (and to everyone else) that I could handle the responsibilities of life on my own.

I took a more professional attitude towards my career, and it proved to pay off. I was in great demand, not only for photography assignments, but also for TV. My American success led to work in Europe and I began accepting assignments there.

I can't say I didn't have some moments of self-doubt. I was a divorcée—and a none too sophisticated one at the time—with a young son to raise. If ever my budding 29 Forever spirit was put to the test, it was then. Happily, I passed with flying colors. When the butterflies would start chasing each other around inside my tummy, I would take a deep breath and refuse to give in to what Little Orphan Annie used to call the whim-whams. Having my child with me was more than a little help. Concentrating on someone you love always works wonders.

9

Little David and I set out to discover the magic of New York. Weekends we scooted in and out of the Museum of Natural History, one of his all-time favorite places. Since he adored automobiles and boats, we took in every auto and boat show at Madison Square Garden. I adore antiques and so when the Garden had an antique fair, I'd turn up with David by the hand, knowing that this was a fun way to teach him respect for other places and other times.

Still, I was a woman alone and I didn't much care for that. Then I met Steve Baker at a photographer's party. The place was awash with models. I hadn't planned to attend; I'd been working all day and had a full day's schedule ahead of me. I phoned the photographer and told him I just couldn't make it. He joked and pleaded and insisted—and I gave in. I went, and met Steve—a very tall, Lincolnesque type, whose faint accent was the only clue to his Budapest origin. He was in advertising and well known as one of its most creative talents. We talked for a long time. He practically exploded with ideas and I found him fascinating and inspiring. He had just created a sensational advertising campaign, "Let Your Fingers Do the Walking," for AT&T. I was intrigued. And furthermore, he seemed to be interested in me as a person and not simply as another blonde model. So many men I'd met talked down to me, peppering their conversation with lush compliments. They seemed to feel that that was expected of them. Or, perhaps, it was just so much easier than digging down and dealing with the person beneath the tall-cool-blonde exterior.

Steve and I began to meet for lunch, when I could squeeze it in between bookings. Then, after a few months, we graduated to cocktails after five. Nothing romantic; he wasn't my type. He seemed much too serious and much too hard to please. But he was different from any man I had ever known. He was, therefore, something of a challenge; and the 29 Forever in me responded. Soon we graduated from cocktails after five to dinner and after-theatre suppers. I can't remember Steve's asking me to marry him; he just assumed that I would. And I did.

We lived in a triplex penthouse with a wrap-around terrace and a fabulous view of the East River. One day in 1963 we loaned our apartment to a Broadway producer to use for a "reading" of a musical play, for which he was trying to raise production money. The living room was a wall-to-wall crush of people, and eventually I found myself in a conversation with one man...

"...and you would be our Food, Fashion, and Beauty Editor," he was saying, assuming that I had heard what preceded this. I hadn't. So he thoughtfully repeated himself: New York was then in the throes of a citywide newspaper strike, but the unions involved had agreed that his East Side "weekly" could become a "daily" for the duration of the strike. A fantastic opportunity, but now he desperately needed someone capable of putting out a two-page spread, five days a week, on Food, Fashion, and Beauty. Was I interested? The 29 Forever in me responded on cue. But I remained cool.

"Why me?" I asked.

"Because I understand you have a five-year-old son and you look nineteen. You must know something a lot of other women don't."

Naturally I accepted. I still couldn't spell, but no matter. I just couldn't miss this opportunity.

For the next three months, I worked perhaps harder than I ever have in my life. But I relished the challenge. I adored the work of being an editor, which I had to do mostly at night. Being both a busy model and an editor was a terrific workload. But, no matter. This was a fresh new experience.

A few years later, while reminiscing with Steve about my "crash" career as a newspaper editor, he said, "You know, you should write a book." Since he had written eight books himself, I thought about it seriously. My 29 Forever spirit flamed again. Early the next morning, before breakfast and before the sun had quite made up its mind to shine, I slipped downstairs, rolled a sheet of paper into our raspberry-colored portable, and began my first book, *The Models' Way to Beauty, Slenderness, and Glowing Health.*

Now, my career is *ideas*. I am still modeling, but only to sell my own products. I am painting, exhibiting, and selling my artwork; I have designed jewelry and men's clothes; and before you read this, my cosmetics will be on the market. This is my fourth book, with a fifth already in its gestation period.

I'm a semibachelor girl again. Steve and I are living apart. We still see each other, and I am still in awe of his creativity. He inspired me to write books and negotiated my first contract with a publisher. We're friends—good friends—and always will be.

But recently when someone asked me if I ever remember having failed at anything I really wanted to do, I honestly couldn't think of any failures. So I asked Steve to help me think of some things I have failed at. He promptly said, "Marriage." I replied that I didn't look at it that way; I prefer to call it not failure, but *progress*—again, that 29 Forever spirit. It refuses to let you dwell on failure. If you have it, you're optimistic. You're looking to the future—to the next opportunity, next experience, next challenge. You *feel* 29. So you *are* 29. Everything good is still ahead of you.

It seems to me that a woman's creativity, productivity, *and* glamour increase with her chronological age, and the world is full of dazzling women who support that theory.

Sophia Loren and Brigitte Bardot are in their forties. And so are Joanne Woodward and Jacqueline Onassis. Zsa Zsa Gabor is...well, she was "Miss Hungary" of 1935, so you figure it out. Ingrid Bergman is approaching sixty. Joan Crawford and Bette Davis are sixty-eight. Claudette Colbert is nearly seventy. Glamourous Gloria Swanson, seventy-six and a great-grandmother, is still a working actress and, most recently, a bride. The deliciously witty Anita Loos, past eighty, published another best seller, while a second musical version of her classic *Gentlemen Prefer Blondes* (with Carol Channing, at fifty-one, playing Lorelei Lee just as she did twenty-five years earlier) poured more gold into her bank account. *Fascinating women. Active women.* They've all got the 29 Forever spirit.

Now, how about *you?* Membership in the 29

Forever Club is open to any woman, regardless of age, income, marital status, or color of hair. *Join.* Become a life member—and in the pages that follow, I'll show you how to do exactly that.

So turn this page, and start right in...

2

Know Thyself
... Love Thyself!

IT'S MY CONTENTION that if you're positively "fizzing" with good health—mental and physical—you're halfway toward your goal of 29 Forever. Hooray for makeup! Three cheers for exercise! BUT even that dynamic combination won't turn the trick unless you have the proper mental attitude *plus* a body properly tuned up and in shipshape.

As far as mental attitude goes, Norman Vincent Peale most certainly knew what he was writing about when he titled his inspiring best seller *The Power of Positive Thinking*. We can also try another variation on that theme: *Think Young*. Take that a step further and *Think* 29 ... Forever.

Why 29? Why not, say, twenty-seven ... twenty-five ... even twenty-two? Because 29 is such an attractive age, both physically and mentally. It's young, but not ingenue young. At 29 you are (hopefully) experienced in the ways of the world and have some notion of who you are and what you want out of life. You're old enough to have learned from your experiences, but you aren't jaded. Never pessimistic. You still believe that another great adventure is just around the corner. At 29, you're sensuous and appealing; you've come to terms with your own sexuality. At 29, you're buoyantly healthy—mentally, physically, and sexually. You're at your peak—if you want to be. 29 Forever starts right there in your lively head.

According to Dr. Walter Brooks McDaniel, if you keep thinking young, it's impossible to grow old. And he should know. The good doctor is the oldest living Harvard graduate. A mere stripling of 103 years, he once taught the patrician likes of Franklin Delano Roosevelt the intricacies of Latin. Dr. McDaniel also makes it a habit never to take any of his worries to bed with him. And neither should you. Tension and depression share an effect in common: they sag your spirits and help ruin your looks. In fact, one of the most important things in keeping one's good looks is relief from tension.

Past eighty, Rose Kennedy is still a stunning-looking woman, and a vast amount of her eye appeal has to do with her serenity. She believes that keeping serene and tranquil under difficult conditions is of the utmost importance.

As for depression (and her sister, self-pity), kick the habit. If you're "addicted," find out what you're feeling so sorry about and, for heaven's sake, *do* something about it! While you are, please don't grit your teeth with determination, but open your pretty mouth and s-m-i-l-e. Be *charming*. Think outside yourself. So what if you're riddled with problems and feeling mushy with self-pity? If you're doing something about it, you should feel proud of yourself. So project good cheer and you'll find that people will react to those vibes and smile right back at you. Guaranteed result: You will feel more upbeat and much more capable of kicking the *Poor Me* syndrome.

Be charming. *Look* charming. Back up that smiling countenance and upbeat personality with a spic 'n' span look from head to toe. I maintain you simply can't feel depressed for very long when you know you look absolutely smashing. A lady I know, who looks perfectly lovely at age eighty-nine (you'd never know she had money worries and has had two very serious operations), advises anyone who will listen, "Whatever you do, you must keep the beauty of your style." Her own face is always made up with great care, and every white hair is lovingly in place. Now it certainly isn't essential that each time you show your face in public that it be fully made up, but a tiny bit of care can go a long way. Never go out of the house unless you're looking fresh and neat. So with that in mind, take heed, and...

Never, ever wear curlers in public. You just know that a woman with a head full of curlers doesn't really believe that another great adventure is just around the corner.

Never, ever chew gum in public. Gum-chewing is marvelous exercise to ward off or correct a droopy chinline, but—like toe-touching—it's not meant to be performed in public.

Never, ever venture outdoors with nails that cry for a manicure. The 29 Forever female starts each day ready, willing, and able to make it the best day ever. She's always impeccably turned out . . . right down to her fingertips.

Now that you've positioned your head, let's give you some simple health tips that come to us via the researchers at the California State Health Department, who tallied them up after an intensive eight-year study:

1) *Don't smoke cigarettes.* They're not only poison to your lungs, but also your heart, and according to the latest scientific data, your skin as well. The skin of the smoker invariably wrinkles earlier than the skin of nonsmokers.

2) *Don't drink excessively.* When I was growing up, there was no liquor kept in our house. Consequently I never had the chance to get used to it. And I shall always remember when, many years ago, I was slightly anemic my doctor gave me a B-12 shot. He said, "Now don't drink any liquor tonight because even one glass will counteract the shot I gave you." See now why your energy level is so much lower the day after you've imbibed so freely? Add to that the fact that cocktails are loaded with calories. Is it worth it? I say No. I'm far happier—and healthier—with an occasional glass of wine.

3) *Don't skip breakfast.* How you start your day determines in a large measure the kind of day you'll have.

4) *Maintain regular and moderate eating habits.* That's so obvious, I have nothing to add.

5) *Keep your weight in proportion to your height.* Dr. Leslie S. Libow, chief of geriatric medicine at Mount Sinai Hospital Services in Elmhurst, New York, says, "If you keep your weight

normal, you'll not only look younger but you may retard other aging symptoms such as diabetes, high blood pressure, or hardening of the arteries."

6) *Sleep at least seven but no more than eight hours per night.* And use only one flat pillow; two will encourage a double chin. In fact, I recommend a tiny baby pillow. It will help stretch your neck muscles.

7) *Get moderate exercise.* In fact, exercise should be as much a habit as sleeping. For it revs up the circulation and can actually heighten mental awareness.

I find that Happiness and Health (physical and mental) inevitably go together. Happy people seem to age more slowly than unhappy people. They appear to have better-looking complexions, better posture; their bones even seem to heal faster than those of unhappy, down-in-the-mouth people. No one is born happy. Happiness is an *achievement*. Calm, serene happiness—the kind that lasts, that takes the knocks and bubbles back to the top again—is *learned*. How? By living the most active, interesting life you can manage. A life where there's not even a tiny corner that Boredom can settle in. I say, *Refuse to be bored.* Boredom will age anyone almost as quickly as a lopsided diet combined with lack of exercise. It's a beauty killer. No doubt about it. I'm with Timothy Dwight who, when he was president of Yale University, said, "The happiest person is the person who thinks the most interesting thoughts."

A recent study, commissioned by the National Institute of Health, on the health and well-being of men places emphasis on the value of what the researchers call "a complex and variable life." I see no reason why this shouldn't also apply to women, do you? *Any* person who sets goals and aims for them is looking to the future and, consequently, is certain to feel, act, and look younger than someone who has settled down into a routine, sedentary life. Age, I believe, is a matter of spirit, not chronology.

In an interview appearing in *W,* the super chic newspaper published by *Women's Wear Daily,* Rose Kennedy rated mental stimulation "essential . . . especially as one gets older. I read a lot, keep up with current events, with my French."

In the same edition, Cristina Ford said, "You can't be beautiful with a sluggish mind. What keeps you young is a change of scene and pace, some recreation that stimulates the brain as well as the body. Too much of the same routine, and you let yourself go."

A handsome woman I know, who is in her late eighties, counsels her friends that, if they want to remain youthful, they must "stay out of ruts. Find something you did when you were young— whatever you loved, sewing or cooking or painting—and concentrate on it." She practices what she preaches. She loved to dance when she was young; in fact, she studied under Vernon Castle, the famous ballroom dancer of the pre- and post-World War I era. So these days she visits centers for the aged in her community and dances for what she calls her "elderly young," also showing them exercises that they can do to keep their bodies limber.

I recommend very highly a book titled *Ageless Aging* by Ruth Winter (Crown Publishers, 1973). Ms. Winter has this to say on the subject of aging:

"What we call aging is not the same for everyone. We all know people of forty who are old and people of eighty who are young. In fact, geriatricians cannot examine a person whose age is unknown and, with any assurance, determine that the person is thirty, fifty, or sixty years old. They may miss by as much as fifteen years."

A snappy octogenarian friend of mine says, "I'm too interested in the things I'm doing to have time to be old." The "things" she's doing? Well, for one thing she's a professional storyteller, a career she began when her husband died about twenty years ago. Every month "rain, blizzard, or shine," she travels around to women's clubs, colleges, and church groups, telling legends and folk tales from memory. And she has some eighty-five enchanting stories committed to memory.

I know another tiny dynamo in her seventies who is so cheery she seems to move in sunshine. This lady works as a volunteer two days a week with ghetto youngsters. She walks to and from her work—a distance of three miles. When the summer sets in and the youngsters scatter, so does she. She heads abroad and spends nine weeks traveling around foreign parts on a bus. "There's no such thing as old age," she maintains, "when your mind is busy."

I have still another friend who, at seventy-eight, is taking piano lessons. A former businesswoman, she retired at seventy-four. She admits that was a mistake. "I retired too young."

I believe that the woman who never seems to look very much older is the woman who has discovered—and maintained—a rhythm that is right for her. A kind of *inner balance*. This means that she sleeps

21

enough, eats and drinks the right amount of calories for her body, and exercises as a matter of course to look and feel lithe. She cares about herself because she knows who she is and she likes—yes, *loves*—who she is. She accepts herself wholeheartedly, and that leaves her free to accept others just as wholeheartedly. (And as my friend who dances for her "elderly young" puts it, "Love, after all swings the world.")

She is always alert . . . tension-free . . . interested . . . and intensely curious about what is happening around her—rather than what is happening *to* her. She is thinking and, consequently, living, outside herself. She's in the real world and she's the richer for it . . . and vice-versa.

Naturally a woman like that is 29 Forever.

I recently came across a poem by R. D. Laing that describes perfectly what it is like to live *without* the 29 Forever spirit:

never	saw it
never	heard it
never	smelt it, touched it, or tasted it
never	felt it
never	heard it mentioned
never	had any idea of it
never	dreamt of it
never	wanted it
never	missed it

is there a problem?

I can't imagine a woman who wouldn't choose to be 29 Forever!

3

The Skin Game

WHILE 29 FOREVER is an attitude, a philosophy, a proud-to-be-Me appearance is part of it, too. You simply can't be 29 Forever if your complexion isn't clear and fresh looking. And it distresses me that so many women know so little about their skin. Ask most women—especially those over thirty—what type skin they have and the answer almost always comes back loud and clear: DRY. It's not always true, of course. But since we know that, as the calendar years add up, one's skin does lose moisture and become drier (and the drier the skin, the more it tends to wrinkle), by age thirty most of us are *convinced* we have dry skin.

Furthermore, almost everything you do *does* dry your skin. Your face is the least protected part of you. It's just *there*...unprotected...constantly exposed to drying wind, drying sunlight, and all the sticky, suffocating grit and chemicals in our polluted air. Sound grim? It is. Unless, of course, you counterattack with a sensible program of facial skin care.

I believe Princess Diane von Furstenberg, a New York-based business woman and celebrated international beauty, summed it all up when she said that skin is so very important because unlike a dress, which you can get rid of and get a new one, "you can't get a new skin as easily."

So take heed and take care of yours. It's the only skin you've got. No tradein possible. Decide right now that you want the look of great, glowing health that only a clear, incredibly moist, smooth skin can give you.

To begin with, it is absolutely essential that you know your skin type so you will be able to give it the lovingly meticulous care it so rightly deserves. Happily it's never too late to improve your skin because, complicated though the skin is, it responds to programmed care. So if you get enough sleep, eat sensibly, drink plenty of water, and exercise daily, you are on your way to a beautiful complexion.

Besides misjudging your skin type, you may also be one of those women who thinks that her skin type is set for life. *Not so.* Your skin is influenced by any number of factors: diet, the climate in which you live, your age. These factors can and do change and, as a result, so does your skin. Certainly, when a woman begins her menopause, her skin (and body) can change. So, when you see a woman of fifty and up who looks sensational, there's a good chance she has been to her doctor and made certain she is getting her fair share of estrogen. You might ask your own doctor for an opinion on this.

To determine your skin type, please answer these six very basic questions:

1) My pores are (a) visible; (b) nearly visible; (c) large and highly visible.

2) My complexion is (a) always shiny; (b) oily in some places; (c) dry and sometimes flaky.

3) I have blemishes (a) often; (b) very rarely; (c) occasionally.

4) After I put on my makeup in the morning (a) my face is oily in a matter of minutes; (b) my face is oily about twelve noon; (c) my makeup doesn't run, but it does appear to fade away.

5) I must shampoo my hair (a) every other day; (b) at least every four days; (c) once a week.

6) I am (a) under 20; (b) 20 to 30; (c) 30-plus.

Have you finished the questions?

All right then, if at least four out of six of your answers were (c)—you definitely have DRY skin.

If, on the other hand, at least four out of six of your answers were (a)—you definitely have OILY skin.

Your answers don't fit into either category? Then you have a COMBINATION skin which means you have both *dry* and *oily* areas.

If your skin is fine textured . . . appears to have no visible pores . . . feels smooth and doesn't shine or have a feel of oiliness—*Congratulations!* You have what is called NORMAL skin and that, my dear, is sheer heaven and practically unheard of.

But even if those six simple questions still leave you unconvinced as to what skin type you have, here's a no-fault test guaranteed to evaporate even the tiniest whisper of doubt:

1) Wash your face thoroughly, pat dry, and wait half an hour.

2) Next, take three pieces of tissue or cigarette paper and mark them A, B, and C.

3) Wipe paper A over your forehead. Wipe paper B over your nose and chin. Wipe paper C over each cheek.

4) Now tally up the results. If tissue is unstained, your skin is dry in that area; some dampness means skin has normal moisture; and traces of oil mean those glands are overactive.

If Your Complexion Is Dry

More fair-haired women have dry skin than dark-haired women. Still you don't have to be a golden blonde with milky-white skin to have dry skin. We all know women with black hair who have thin, fine complexions that seem to start to freckle, fry, and dry at the mere mention of SUN. So no matter what your age or coloring, the only thing you need to know is: if you have dry skin, you must take special care to give it the *loving* care it needs to avoid wrinkles. I know, because I come from a long line of dry-skinned females. My mother's skin would freckle if it was exposed to light for even a few minutes. And imagine, she lives in sunny Florida! Still her complexion is lovely—freckle-free and healthy. She simply won't have it any other way.

So let's start at the beginning, where every woman should start regardless of skin type, with an impeccably deep-down clean skin. Now some women believe that the only way to get that clean a skin is with soap and water. But I maintain that even if a woman has very oily skin, it shouldn't be subjected to the drying effects of soap—even a super-fatted soap. I regard soap as a Beauty Killer, particularly for dry skin. Most soaps have a lye base and are scented with perfume. Both ingredients rob the skin of oil and moisture. I *never* put soap of any kind on my face and, at forty-two, I have a great complexion.

Here is the protect 'n' pamper skin care program I follow for dry skin:

Each morning and each evening before retiring, I apply baby oil all over my face and neck. With tissues and my fingertips—using what I call my Up-and-Out motion—I cleanse once and then again. Once is decidedly not enough. (Of course when I repeat the cleansing, I use clean tissues.) Then, when I'm convinced (white tissues make it perfectly clear) my skin is deep-down clean, I apply a liquid moisturizer to my face and neck. A night cream isn't always necessary, as a light moisturizer will often give dry skin all the lubrication it needs, but you need an extra-rich cream during the very drying winter months, and after age thirty.

But if, despite your dry skin and my please-don't advice, you feel you *must* apply soap and water, then in place of the second application of baby oil I suggest you use a bland soap and warm water (*not* hot, it's drying). Dry skin is both sensitive and fragile, so don't scrub it with a washcloth—use your fingertips. By all means, your dry skin should be kept well moisturized all day long. A good moisturizer serves as a protective shield. Never, never apply makeup unless you have first applied a moisturizer. When you apply your moisturizer, take care to pat gently around your eyes and mouth; tiny lines are very apt to crop up here first, because the skin is so very thin in these areas. The very best time to apply a moisturizer is immediately after you have cleansed your complexion. That will seal the pores against impurities.

Facial Masque for Dry Skin

Honey and Egg. Doesn't that sound incredibly rich and nourishing? It should, because it is.

Honey is a natural moisturizer, probably the oldest known to womankind. The egg's natural lecithin and albumen work to refine your skin and give it a better texture, as well as added moisture. Together, honey and egg are a spectacular combination. Furthermore, this masque is so simple to prepare.

Beat together one egg yolk (*not* egg white, that's drying) and one tablespoon of strained honey. Using your fingertips, apply the mixture all over your just-cleansed face and throat. Let it remain on for fifteen to twenty minutes (no longer), and then remove with a towel, moistened with lukewarm water. I suggest you reapply your honey and egg masque once every two weeks.

Foods for Dry Skin

Pay special attention to your intake of Vitamin B. That is, milk...yogurt...egg yolk...tomatoes...wheat germ...nuts...whole-grain breads. Besides nourishing dry skin, Vitamin B also helps relieve tension which aggravates a dry skin condition. (Beauty czarina Estée Lauder confides that she eats a pat of butter a day, "because it lubricates the skin.")

Vitamin D is important, too. Cod-liver oil capsules are a good year 'round source of this vitamin.

Postscript for Dry Skin

Pay extra-special attention to your skin during the winter months. Cold, blustery weather causes severe moisture depletion. Think for a moment: you move from a steam-heated room *(drying)* into the freezing outdoors *(drying),* and then back into a steam-heated room *(drying).* You are literally zigzagging between two extremes of temperature, both of which are m-u-r-d-e-r for dry skin. I can't urge you enough to invest in a room humidifier for your bedroom, so your skin can be absorbing moisture while you are sleeping.

If Your Complexion Is Oily

Begin and end each day by wetting your face and neck with water and then, with your fingertips and my Up-and-Out motion, massage a deep-cleansing, nongreasy lotion into your skin. Rinse off with warm water and then finish with lukewarm water. Pat dry with a soft towel. Next, saturate a cotton pad with an astringent toning lotion (witch hazel will do just fine); it will reduce oiliness and help refine those too-prominent pores that are a telltale sign of an oily skin condition.

Please don't think that just because your skin is oily you don't need a moisturizer. The skin around your eyes and neck needs moisture. This is especially true in wintertime. But a note of caution:

it is possible to overdry the outer layer of an oily skin. This can only be corrected by using the correct moisturizer which, for your skin type, is a light moisturizer; fatty ones, obviously, aren't for you.

Once or twice a week, you should treat your skin to the detergent action of *cleansing grains*. Now and then, switch from the grains to a *medicated* soap (which I don't really place in the soap category), working it up to a full lather via hot water and a fairly rough washcloth. Make sure you allow the lather to dry on your skin before you start to scrub (and, of course, scrub only the oiliest places). Rinse with cold water, and then finish with a brisk astringent to tighten pores (again, witch hazel will do just fine, but if you want to get positively back-to-nature about it, you might try cucumber juice).

Facial Masque for Oily Skin

Oatmeal. It's perfectly marvelous for an oily skin. All you do is make a paste of dry oatmeal and warm water. Then pat it on and let it dry. Just as soon as it's dry, rinse off with clear, cold water. Follow up with a generous splash of your favorite skin freshener. I suggest you apply your oatmeal masque two or three times a week.

Foods for Oily Skin

Like your dry-skinned sisters, you must be sure to get your supply of the versatile Vitamin B. A shortage of Vitamin B aggravates an oily skin condition, just as it does a dry skin condition, in your case by increasing the flow of your already overactive skin oils. Skip the nuts, however, and instead concentrate on those delicious fruit-flavored yogurts, and when it comes to milk, make it fat free.

Get your fair share of Vitamin A, too: spinach...calf's liver...eggs...cantaloupe...carrots ...yellow corn. Hungarian-born Julie Sans is not only a skin care specialist, but a trained nutritionist as well, and she says, "The trouble is that most people don't eat enough green vegetables, especially dandelion greens. Some of the healthiest children in the world come from the heel of Italy, where poor families literally live on them."

Postscript for Oily Skin

Don't, under any circumstances, apply steam to your face. You may be tempted if your skin is exceptionally oily, but please don't. Intense heat applied directly to the face is much *too* drying.

Tuck handy little astringent pads in your handbag and use them during the day.

Avoid fried foods and highly seasoned foods, both of which can cause an oversecretion of oil in your pores.

Don't use any greasy beauty products on your face.

Don't use pancake makeup. It's too drying, even for oily skin and, furthermore, it clogs pores.

If Your Complexion is a Combination of Dry and Oily

Special measures must be taken. Cleanse the oily sections more often than the dry sections, and treat those dry patches for what they are: dry skin. In other words, use the preparations for oily and dry skin on the appropriate parts of your face and neck.

Facial Masques for Combination Skin

1) Honey. Honey is all you need for this masque, and here is how you apply it (remembering, of course, that a masque is applied only to a super-clean complexion):

Take a tablespoon of pure, strained honey that is at room temperature and apply it all over face and neck with your fingertips. Sticky? You bet it is. So you must be very, very gentle as you apply it to the delicate skin around your eyes. You actually massage the honey into your skin by pressing your fingers onto your skin and then pulling them away quickly. Leave your honey masque on for fifteen minutes, then remove it with a warm towel pressed over your face and neck. Once the masque is off, follow up *immediately* with a towel dipped in cold water. Where your skin is dry, finish with a lubricating lotion. Where your skin is oily, use your skin freshener.

2) Egg. Separate the egg carefully and work each part into a gentle froth. With fingertips, apply the white to the oilier areas of your complexion and

the yolk to the rest. Let set for fifteen minutes. Remove with a few splashes of cool water so the yolk doesn't curdle. An egg masque is a delightful once-a-week beauty experience.

Foods for Combination Skin

Since you quite literally have two different skin conditions, you must follow a balanced diet. Get your fair share of Vitamins A and B, both of which are essential to complexion beauty no matter what your skin type.

If Your Complexion Is Normal

... Mine is green with envy. Still, don't let your good fortune go to your head and start taking your soft, dewy-fresh complexion for granted. And don't be tempted to experiment with gooey face creams or facial masques that dry your skin, simply because you've passed your thirtieth birthday. Cleanse your skin twice daily and follow with a light moisturizer. That's all you really need, except at those times when you're exposed to extreme weather conditions.

No Matter What Your Skin Type

Drink eight glasses (certainly never less than six) of water every day. Water is a beauty tonic, the most natural drink skin can have, and one it simply can't live without. Water is a natural purifier that washes you internally and keeps your skin smooth, elastic, and moisturized from within. In short, water can work wonders for you!

Your Body Complexion

I'll never understand why it is still common practice to think only of the face when using the word *complexion*. Some women even stop at the chin line and refuse to include the neck! Well, when I say *complexion* I really mean from the face right down to the feet. The skin from stem to stern, as it were. And so to make that point, I refer to your *body complexion*. I want it to look and feel as soft, smooth, and dewy fresh as your face. Don't you?

There is no finer prescription for a beautiful allover complexion than a sumptuous, hot tub. To me a bath is balm for mind and soul as well as the body. I soak and let my mind go blissfully blank. As a result, my bath is both a great relaxer and revitalizer.

Mala Rubinstein says, "Relaxation is vital to

everybody's beauty, and everybody should find their own way to relax."

For Polly Bergen, the dynamic actress-singer and now a successful cosmetician, her way to relax is to bathe. "I bathe every night for cleanliness and sensuality," she says. "It's a beautiful moment."

French-born Pauline Trigère, the famous fashion designer, says, "My bath is my joy and relaxation. It's where I revive. When I get home, tired and rushed, and have to go out again for the evening, I don't take a B-12 shot—I take a bath."

Smart women the world over adore their baths. Some English beauties pamper their allover pink-and-white complexions by adding seaweed to their baths.

On the chic Italian island of Ischia, titled beauties swear by mud baths.

In Finland, home of the sauna, those ravishing Finnish blondes are said to bathe in camomile.

And in certain islands off the coast of Japan, where the sands are heated by underground steam, I hear the ladies favor a sand bath.

But wherever they are, it's a slow, lazy bath and not a fast 'n' frisky shower that appeals to them.

Now here is my every-night bath ritual:

I start by slowing down. I purposely begin to move in what practically amounts to slow motion. (And to make certain nothing will snap me out of my self-induced reverie, I take my phone off the hook.) Then I prepare a glass of iced tea or a freshly squeezed iced juice. I bring the glass into the bathroom and I start the hot water pouring into the tub. While the water is pouring lightly—continuously—I add a few drops of a fragrantly

36

scented bubble bath. While the hot water and the
scented bubbles are mixing together in the tub
(bubble baths soften water), I begin to remove my
makeup slowly, deliberately.

When my facial complexion looks and feels
scrupulously clean, I step into my tub—first putting
my bottle of baby oil and my glass of tea or juice
both within easy reach—and I just laze there up to
my shoulders in hot water and sparkling bubbles.
Once I feel thoroughly relaxed and awfully, awfully
good about myself and the world at large, I begin to
wash myself from the shoulders down with a gentle
soap and a soft washcloth.

When I'm finished, I put the used soapy cloth in
the sink and lie back again, just lolling there in the
water, reaching out for my cold drink and sipping it
ever so slowly. Soon I start to perspire. I continue to
sip and relax, and perhaps fifteen to twenty minutes
go by. (No more than twenty, however; too much
time in a hot tub can be fatiguing.) I close my eyes;
and sometimes I have my radio or record player
going so that I hear soothing, romantic music.

Now I reach out for my bottle of baby oil...tip
in a few drops...turn the hot water off...and
slowly massage some of the now lightly oiled water
into my body. *Heaven!* I feel so incredibly moist,
marvelous, and relaxed; nothing can match this for
pure sensuality.

I step out of the tub and proceed to gently towel
myself dry.

A fluffy bubble bath without the baby oil is
recommended if you have an oily body complexion.
A milk bath is sheer luxury for all types of skin,
whipping your tub water into a creamy foam. You

can buy a packet of powdered skim milk at your supermarket and pour it directly into your bath water while the water is still running. But if you do use regular skim milk, you must rinse with clear water. Rinsing isn't necessary if you prefer to use one of the readymade milk bath powders available at drug and department stores.

Body Complexion Groomers

Loofah is a soapy string of vegetable sponge that is used for scrubbing away dead skin, while leaving your body feeling all atingle. A natural loofah is about fifteen inches long. You might try a loofah glove for spot cleaning. Models, who must bare their backs to an all-seeing camera in the course of a fashion sitting, invariably give their backs a good scrub with a loofah every two weeks or so. But *do* remember, scrubbing is drying. So if you have dry skin, use a body moisturizer after the scrub. A few drops of baby oil will do.

If you should decide that a loofah is too much for your sensitive skin, you might want to try a friction strap made of hemp. Or a long-handled body brush made of stiff, long, natural bristles that will tone up the circulation on your arms and legs as well as your back.

Certainly any woman who aspires to be 29 Forever should own a pumice stone, a magical piece of ultraporous volcanic lava that rubs away dry, flaky skin on elbows and heels and leaves them looking and feeling deliciously soft, smooth, and moist.

A Final Après-Tub Touch

Rub yourself all over with a moisturizer or light oil (baby oil), and I do mean *all over*. Including your feet. If you have an oily body complexion, use a pushbutton powder or talc spray for a gloriously smooth and sleek feeling.

To further enhance your relaxation in the tub, consider glamourizing your bathroom. Paint it a sensuous color. Invest in a vinyl pillow and tray of the same color so that you can settle back in the tub and read or sip tea and nibble a biscuit if you want to. Fill your bathroom with plants; they thrive in that atmosphere, nourished by moisture and steam. Just imagine a bathroom with sunny yellow walls...a ceiling the color of a summer sky...a profusion of green plants. Why, it would be the closest thing to lolling in a Caribbean sea. Add a few bars of soothing music. After that, tuck yourself into bed and s-l-e-e-p.

Block That Sun!

If you're going to win the Skin Game, you're going to have to become very aware of the sun. If there's a primary rule to play by, it's *block that sun!*

How? The best strategy is to *shun the sun completely*. Play it cool and slip into something light and airy. Wear a wide-brimmed hat to shade your face; and make sure that your face is wearing a sun block cream under your makeup. If that's not possible—or if you have a smashing new bikini that can't withstand the lure of sun and surf—then play it smart. Apply a sun block lotion or cream from head to toe. Yes, even on a cloudy or hazy day, since the sun's ultraviolet rays (which do the damage) can burn your skin even then. Some light always gets through and *all* light exposure is harmful to the skin.

Aileen Mehle, who under the pen name "Suzy" writes a nationally syndicated society column and frequents the world's chicest spas, never goes into the sun. She used to sunbathe a lot, but one day some years ago while vacationing abroad, she saw dark blotches on her chest and consulted a dermatologist at once. He told her to stay out of the sun, and she has ever since.

If you must be further convinced as to how really damaging exposure to the sun can be, it's the opinion of Dr. Albert Kleigman, professor of dermatology at the University of Pennsylvania, that most of the so-called signs of aging—wrinkled, leathery, sagging skin—are caused less by the passage of time than by exposure, year in and out, to the sun. Dr. Cyril Marsh, eminent New York dermatologist, estimates that 50 percent or more of the aging that occurs to the skin over the years is due to the sun.

Skin care expert Georgette Klinger, whose client list reads like the *Who's Who* of the Beautiful People, believes that when you're thirty or more, you should avoid the sun completely. Good advice. But I say no matter what age you are, shun the sun. For everything you do in your teens and twenties affects how you'll look at forty and fifty.

Fair skin, of course, is the most susceptible; particularly skin with a tendency to freckle. But even black skin is not completely immune to sun damage.

Dr. Bedford Shelmire, Jr., in his fine book *The Art of Looking Younger* (St. Martin's Press, 1973) advises, "A few months of intense sun exposure can produce more aging changes than a century of normal wear. Sunlight is capable of penetrating the skin; it affects not only the surface but also the living tissues of both layers."

So it's up to you to protect yourself against this damage. It is certainly one of the most important parts of preventive skin care. There is nothing narcissistic about caring for your skin. A healthy, beautiful complexion isn't a miracle. It's an *accomplishment*.

It's interesting, I think, how women's attitudes toward exposure to the sun has changed with time. Back in the Victorian era, a tan was considered *unchic*. Workers in the fields were exposed to the harsh sunlight and they looked it: skins like hides, with squint lines zigzagging from their eyes and deep creases encircling their necks, like the age lines on the bark of a tree. But the so-called quality folk opted for the pale look—proof that they had the means, as well as the good sense, to stay out of the sun. (An 1899 issue of *Ladies' Home Journal,* for example, advised readers, "Never go out in blustery weather without a veil unless you wish a tanned skin or freckles.")

Then it would seem, as more and more women became flappers and bobbed their hair and took paying jobs, a suntan took on the stature of a status symbol. A toasty look seemed to say that, though she was a working girl—a member of the proud working class—she nevertheless had both the time and the means to get outdoors and play. Naturally enough, a *winter* tan was très chic!

Now, happily, women are growing wiser. They are learning that there is nothing good about the sun on their skin.

Bear in mind, too, that surfing isn't the only time you're exposed to the sun. The tennis court, the golf course, and the ski slope are other fun spots that are sun spots. Dinah Shore, a really superb tennis player, never fails to wear a visored hat while on the court as well as a sun block under her makeup. Double protection!

If, for one reason or another, you and your natural enemy—the sun—are going to have to get together, please follow these rules for self-preservation:

1) Do your level best to stay out of the sun between 10 A.M. and 2 P.M. That's the time the sun is at its strongest. It peaks at noon, so if you must expose yourself, do it in early morning or late afternoon.

2) Your sun block lotion or cream should contain PABA (paraaminobenzoic acid) a substance that is tops when it comes to blocking out those beastly ultraviolet rays. Remember that swimming and perspiration will wash off your sun block. Keep reapplying it from time to time. You need protection every minute you're in the sun. Yes, even while swimming, because ultraviolet radiation travels *through* water. Keep using your sun block even after you start to get a fairly deep tan, for it's

quite possible to get a painful burn over a tan.

3) No product can work miracles, so it's up to you to read the label carefully. Products designed to give you maximum protection from the sun's rays stress on their labels their filtering qualities and builtin protectors. Some of these products are creams, others are lotions. If the product gives you only limited protection, it will stress fast tanning and deep, long-lasting color. These products are most often an oil or gel; and they're certainly not for a woman with delicate skin.

4) The best way to build up your resistance to the ultraviolet rays is by *gradual* exposure to the sun, starting with a very brief exposure and gradually increasing your sunning time five minutes a day for the first week.

I suggest you follow this time schedule: Fair Skin—a starting time of ten minutes; Medium Skin—fifteen minutes; Dark Skin—twenty minutes. And *don't* just lie there. Keep rotating: first one side, then the other.

5) Sunlight bounces off water and sand. In fact, sand reflects about 50 percent of the sun's burning rays. All of which means that lazing around the pool or sea in the shade of an umbrella offers no real protection. As for the ski country, snow reflects as much as 85 percent of the sun's burning rays.

6) Arm yourself with a really fine pair of sunglasses. By that I mean a pair that's long on protection *and* glamour. Your eyes are supersensitive to the sun. Furthermore, without sunglasses you'll just naturally squint and develop lines around your orbs that will last, even when your tan is a thing of the past.

While we're on the subject of the durability of sun damage—it's *cumulative*. Last year's skin damage doesn't disappear with your tan. The damage clings and gets added on to the next time you're foolish enough to expose yourself unwisely to the sun, until eventually the damage (drying, wrinkling, loss of elasticity) is irreparable.

7) The salt in the ocean and the chemicals in the pool both dry out your skin and leave it thirsting for moisture. Replenish those natural oils that have been evaporating away with a generous coating of your favorite moisturizing lotion. Then seal it in with a satiny layer of refreshing talc.

My Own Suntan Regimen

Sometimes I want a tan. Sometimes—most of the time—I prefer a pale look. But when I want a tan, I also want to protect my skin from sun damage, while at the same time making certain I'm getting the same even, toasty shade from top to bottom. Impossible? Not at all. So if you and Ol' Sol must get together, you might want to try my safe tanning method:

1) I tie my hair up off my neck so that there'll be no streaky pale spot there, and my hair won't get tipped with suntan lotion.

2) I apply my regular tanning lotion from my shoulders down to my feet—yes, soles too.

3) Then I apply my "indoor" tanning lotion— the kind that tans you chemically with or without an assist from the sun—to my face and neck. Of course, I've cleansed my face and neck thoroughly and there's not even the tiniest bit of moisturizer on my skin. I immediately wash my hands with soap, otherwise the "indoor" tanning lotion will stain the palms of my hands. (A second application is recommended if you want a darker tan.)

4) Now, protected top to bottom, I cover my head with a sun hat and head for the sunshine, taking along sunglasses to prevent any squint lines.

5) In the interests of a more even color, I'll remove my sun hat, but for no more than five to ten minutes. Then, back goes the hat. The sunglasses stay where they are—on my face—at all times. I reapply the regular tanning lotion to my body when needed.

6) Of course, I obey all seven of the rules for self-preservation which I've spelled out for you on pages 42-44.

4

Drinking and Smoking:
The Beauty Killers

ONCE UPON A TIME, a teenaged girl's fantasy of *sophistication* was to have a cocktail in one hand and a cigarette in the other. Well all I can say is: once upon a time, it was also thought that the world was flat . . . that if the Lord had wanted man to fly, he'd have given him wings . . . and that menopause meant a woman was over the hill.

Still, we hear today that more and more teenagers are taking to drink, that they're being weaned away from drugs and toward alcohol, which is simply another form of addiction. Adult Americans are setting a deplorable example; it is estimated that we spend $3 *million an hour* on alcohol!

An occasional drink does add to most people's sociability. But in the process it also opens superficial blood vessels; and excessive drinking, therefore, leads to red, blotchy skin and a network of tiny, popped veins. I believe Dr. Robert B. Taylor in *Doctor Taylor's Guide to Healthy Skin for All Ages* (Arlington House, 1974) put it most succinctly when he wrote, "Other than providing seven calories per gram, alcohol serves no useful function...and can only harm healthy skin." In case you think beer doesn't fit into the category of alcohol—a 12 oz. can of beer contains as much alcohol as a cocktail. So the "beer belly" is almost always accompanied by spindly legs as well as a red, blotchy skin, because most heavy drinkers—whether their drink is beer or bourbon—just drink, and rarely eat sensibly.

Drinking ravages a woman's looks. Heavy drinking makes the drinker prone to edema, which causes the body to retain fluid. Result: the skin bloats and stretches, which eventually causes wrinkles. Finally, I ask you, what is sadder and more unattractive than an inebriated female? (Or male?)

Dr. Alfred J. Cantor, author of *Dr. Cantor's Longevity Diet: How to Slow Down Aging and Prolong Youth and Vigor* (Prentice-Hall, 1967), really puts it on the line when he says, "The license to drink is a license to kill—to kill yourself!"

As for the evils of smoking, they are so numerous and so shocking that I'll simply list them and let you decide for yourself whether puffing a cigarette is or is not a damnably foolish thing to do. There are more than 20,000,000 women in America still smoking and most of them are in the twenty-five to forty-four age group—old enough to know better. There are also about 4,000,000 teenage smokers and the most recent statistics indicate that, for the first time in history, the percentage of teenage girls who smoke has almost caught up to that of boys.

So you can imagine how delighted I was to receive the following note from a teen who had just read my first book.

She reported that she had shed 20 pounds by following my advice, had gotten rid of dandruff, "and now I've got so many boy friends and new girl friends that I don't know what to do with all of them." Then she went on to tell me something about her hometown (pop. 982). "In our town the 'in' thing is to smoke and drink. Well, once I read your book, it made me realize that that stuff is bad for you, and if you like YOU and want to live and have a great body and be healthy—that stuff is OUT!"

Of all the "fan mail" that first book of mine attracted, I think that note pleased me the most.

Just as I think Dr. Taylor and Dr. Cantor were very succinct on the subject of drinking, I think glamourous Eva Gabor is equally succinct on the subject of smoking. She thinks smoking is not only dangerous for your health and ruins your skin, but also is very unfeminine as well.

True, and now let's get down to specifics:

• Smoking fills the lungs with up to 300 different compounds of gases, liquid droplets, and other harmful substances.

• Oral cancer is about four times higher in smokers.

• Heavy smokers have twice the death rate of nonsmokers in the 45-54 age bracket.

• Blood of a heavy smoker has lost about one-fifth of its oxygen-carrying capacity. (After a three-year study, a research team from the medical college at the University of Wisconsin concluded that the high carbon monoxide levels in the blood caused by smoking constitute a danger in blood transfusions, and for a patient with a borderline heart condition, the results could be fatal.)

• Nicotine and Vitamin C are incompatible. This means that if you smoke, say, twenty cigarettes a day, you may be suffering from a Vitamin C deficiency; and Vitamin C is essential to the health of your teeth and bones.

• Smoking while pregnant can cause some women to have stillbirths.

• Smoking breeds wrinkles. A heavy smoker of forty often has almost the same number of lines in her face as a nonsmoker of sixty. Why? Smoking constricts the veins, which in turn cuts down circulation. Result? Outer layers of skin become drier.

• Smoking dries out and discolors fingernails.

• Smokers are more prone to headaches than nonsmokers.

• Research shows that respiratory illnesses happen twice as often to young children whose parents smoke at home, compared to those with parents who don't smoke.

• Smoking desensitizes the sense of smell. Flowers wilt in a smoke-filled room. And you can't even appreciate their fragrance before they succumb to the smoke.

• Smoking desensitizes the sense of taste. And dulling of the taste buds inevitably finds the heavy smoker desiring heavily seasoned foods. Consequently if one's skin is oily, it gets oiler.

• The stale odor of cigarettes clings to your hair, your clothes, and your breath; and no amount of seductive perfume or concentrated breath freshener will really hide it. (Romantic, isn't it?)

• Smoking is *not* relaxing. That's a myth. The nicotine in just one cigarette makes your heart beat faster and your blood pressure rise.

I could go on and on. But I'll stop. And you stop—*smoking*. Kick the habit and you'll breathe freely again, have more vitality, look and feel younger—and even smell nicer.

Granted that it isn't all that easy to stop—it requires will power, a shot of common sense, and a few aids. Sugarless gum is one example; many women discover that keeping the mouth occupied is one way to keep the mind off smoking. A fresh new interest also helps, like signing up for a dance class or a session at a gymnasium. It should be something very active that demands concentration.

You don't smoke? Fabulous! Never start. That's one sure way to guarantee that you'll be 29 Forever.

5

About Face!

THERE ISN'T A woman alive who can't be better looking. It's all a matter of learning how. Of course, it should start early, long before you're 29—even before nineteen. It's what I call *preventive care*. After all, it's much more sensible—and simple—to protect what you have than to try to recapture it after it's faded through sheer neglect.

Unlearn Those Damaging
Facial Habits

There's a severe penalty if you don't: a perpetually cross and dejected look that will become yours for keeps. So before these homemade "disfigurements" permanently crease your face and blight your image, an ounce of *preventive* care now will do far more than pounds of cosmetics can after the damage has been done.

Always guard your eyes from sun, wind, and glare with a pair of good sunglasses. Without sunglasses, you'll squint, and squinting encourages wrinkles and frown lines. If you read while outdoors, keep your book, paper, or magazine at an angle that will keep the reading material from reflecting the rays into your eyes. (Sun, by the way, should always be over your right shoulder.)

Have your vision checked at least once a year; and if you need eyeglasses, *get them*. Without them, you'll squint.

It's terribly old fashioned to believe—as women once did—that eyeglasses rob you of glamour. It's practically the reverse today. Women like Gloria Steinem, who wear faintly tinted specs year 'round, have elevated eyeglasses to the status of a bonafide fashion accessory. Many very chic women with 20/20 vision wear "fashion glasses" with clear or lightly tinted lenses—just for fun.

No Frowning Allowed

My sister Francey was once a great frowner; a forehead wrinkler, too. When she was a teenager and hated school homework, she'd put her face in a book and suddenly up would go her forehead and on would come the wrinkles: a protest action if ever I saw it! Well, I showed her how to break those habits with nothing more formidable than a strip of scotch tape.

I scissored a piece of tape just large enough to fit

between her eyebrows; that was for the frown. Then another, somewhat larger splice of tape went across her forehead. At first Francey treated it as a huge joke and got the giggles. But once she gave it a serious try, she was impressed. (Furthermore, I suspect the persistent little tug of the tape each time she frowned or wrinkled her forehead was a lot more pleasant than my nagging.)

Sleep Like a Baby

. . . with a tidy little baby pillow under your head instead of a big clumpy one that, since it props your head up to such an unnatural angle, encourages a double chin. A baby pillow simply supports your neck muscles. It doesn't affect your face in the slightest and that's important; a so-called "normal" size pillow surrounds your face and squeezes it into some pretty ridiculous shapes as you sleep unaware of the peculiar little facial you're receiving. But if you simply won't go the baby pillow route, then at least confine yourself to one fairly flat pillow. Two pillows will *guarantee* you a double chin.

Facial Isometrics

They're not miracleworkers, but they are facesavers. For if the muscles underneath your skin are firm, you'll look young. It's when those little muscles around the nose and mouth sag, when cheeks start to droop, that you no longer look young.

Facial exercises will stimulate circulation and your skin will look smoother, firmer. But it will take time before you see results. It's something like taking gelatine for stronger nails—you have to keep at it. Still, facial isometrics are a lot simpler (and cheaper) than turning yourself over to a plastic surgeon for a few expert tucks.

The basic rule for exercising your face is simple: keep everything UP and BACK. Before you commence your facial exercises, cleanse your skin thoroughly, and then cream it. Facial exercises done when the skin is dry can invite lines. Yes, do these exercises at least once every day.

A Firmer Chin Line

Protrude your bottom lip as far out as it can go. Hold to the slow count of three. Relax. Repeat. Do six repetitions.

Repeat, but this time—after the count of three— waggle your bottom lip in exaggerated fashion from left to right several times. Relax. Repeat. Do six repetitions.

Curl your tongue backward and press it against the roof of your mouth. Press hard. Relax. Do six repetitions.

A More Shapely Mouth

Say the word CHURCH. Say it slowly and exaggerate the "ch" sound. You will feel the peaks of your upper lip rise and curl forward. Help it along. Try to make *both* your lips become rounder and fuller as you say the word. Do ten repetitions.

Imitate the Mona Lisa. That's right, start to smile and then stop it in midair without parting your lips. Try to force the corners of your mouth upward, but don't let them rise. This gentle, but firm, tug-of-war is, in my opinion, very good for lifting the sagging cheek and mouth muscles. Do six repetitions. Rest. Do six more.

For Firmer Cheeks

Place your index finger vertically over the center of your mouth. Now attempt to blow that finger away. The harder you blow, the harder you offer resistance with your finger. This exercise will not only help firm and smooth your cheeks, but will also discourage the vertical lines that all too often begin to form from the corners of your nose down to the corners of your mouth.

The following exercise is a much more complex one, and I suggest that you do it in front of a mirror so that you are certain to have your fingers properly placed:

Place three fingers of your left hand very gently on the right side of your face; that is, from the corner of your right nostril down to the corner of your mouth. Next, *gently* press your right thumb on the outside corner of your right eye, and the remaining fingers of your right hand on the area just above and between your eyebrows. I call these your "control fingers," for they are placed in a way that will prevent lines from forming in tender skin areas as you do this really remarkable facial exercise. Wink your right eye as you lift the right side of your mouth. You WINK and LIFT in unison. *Quickly.* Do this fifty times. Then rest and repeat fifty more times on the left side of your face, with your "control fingers" placed in the same position but, of course, this time on the left side of your face where the winking and lifting are going to take place.

For a Younger Neckline

Remember: your face doesn't end at your chinline. I say your face extends clear down to the base of your throat. Here are two very simple exercises that are simply wonderful for your neckline. Before you start these exercises, have your shoulders bare. I want you to be certain you see the way your neck muscles will flex—even lifting the skin over your breastbone.

1)   Stick your tongue out. Yes, stick it out just as far as it can go, and when it's at its limit—can't go any further—try to curl the tip until you can see it. You won't be able to, of course, but *try.* This exercise will tighten the muscles in the center of your neck. Repeat ten times.

2)   Try to touch the tip of your nose with your *bottom* lip, pushing it up and over your upper lip. Hold bottom lip in this position and tilt head backward and slowly turn head from one side to the other. You will feel the marvelous stretch in your neck muscles. Relax. Repeat ten times.

For Your Eyes

It's very important that you place your "control fingers" properly—and gently—because the skin beneath your eyes is so very thin and delicate.

Place the fingertips of your left hand below the bottom lashes of your left eye, and the fingertips of your right hand below the bottom lashes of your right eye. Gently. *Don't* press. Very slowly lift both lower lids upward, taking special care not to wrinkle your forehead as you do so. Lift both lids as high as you can. Relax, and try again. Do six repetitions.

Give Yourself a Facial

A good facial is still another way to exercise your face. Some areas of your face tend to grow rather lazy. A good facial will stimulate them and keep them resilient, firm, and youthful.

The technique follows the basic rule for all facial exercises: you use upward and outward movements to keep everything UP and BACK. You play on the skin with fingertips, alternately patting and lifting it *gently*. The purpose of a facial is to tone and firm the skin, not to stretch it. And, of course, before your facial you cleanse and cream your complexion.

You start at the collarbone and run your fingers lightly over your throat with a hand-over-hand movement, up and out.

Place the backs of both hands under your chin and flutter the backs of your fingers against your chin, working from the center outward and upward toward your earlobes.

Place your index finger gently from the corner of your mouth to the side of the nostril, along the line that runs from the side of the nostril. With the fingers of your other hand, work the skin in a circular fashion, upward and outward under the cheekbone. Repeat on the other side of the face.

Start at the sides of your nose with your index fingers (thumbs under jawbones); curve your hands up and out in a sweeping motion along the cheekbones and jawbones, all the way up to your hairline. Do not pull or tug at the skin.

With the cushions of your fingers, stroke *gently* over the eye area, working from the inside tip of the eye upward and outward to the eye bone.

Use a circular motion over the forehead, nose, and chin, stimulating but not stretching the skin.

Finish by playing all ten fingers ever so lightly over your entire face, alternately patting and lifting.

6

Corrective Makeup

I REALLY DISLIKE that identifying tag (sounds too much like "orthopedic shoes"), but it does fit. There's nothing at all *preventive* about makeup, but it can certainly be *corrective*. Used with purpose and skill, it can work wonders to play down what is a less than glamourous feature, while playing up your best features.

So don't, for heaven's sake, be timid when it comes to experimenting with makeup. There's a whole colorful world of exciting beauty products out there for you to choose from. *Experiment*. Remember: if your makeup is outdated, you'll look outdated. Skin tone changes with time. The very structure of your face changes. So makeup that was divine at twenty may be deadly at forty.

Here are some general rules for makeup that I believe every woman should consider:

Invest in a blusher for a glow of natural-looking color. Blushers are available in a brushon powder, cream, and liquid.

Keep as much color as possible out of your foundation and powder. Avoid the pink and orangey tones and opt instead for the more natural-looking beige and neutral tones. You can get the color you want via cream rouge. Rouge, by the way, should be worn where the sun would naturally give your complexion a glow: namely cheeks, chin, forehead, perhaps even the neck.

Use a thin liquid foundation. It helps conceal fine lines. Apply it to face and neck with a sponge, and then press a tissue between eyebrows, over and under your mouth, and wherever you may have excess "peach fuzz." This bit with the tissue will prevent your foundation from caking in these cakeable areas. Let's face it: every skin, even very young skin, has fine lines at the corners of the mouth, on the throat, and around the eyes. So, to make sure these fine lines are covered by your foundation, spread the skin of these areas *gently* while applying your foundation.

Invest in a highlight, an off-white coverup that you should apply over your foundation to *any* dark areas of the face; for example, dark circles under the eyes. Believe it or not, that very same highlight can work to strengthen a weak part of your face, too. For example, you can give added character to a weak chin by applying your highlight on and slightly above the jawline—from ear to ear. Smudge it so there is no line of demarcation, and make certain the highlight doesn't go under the chinbone, otherwise you'll defeat its effectiveness.

Pale lipsticks and naturally light lipsticks are NOT the same thing. Pale lipsticks give a chalky, unnatural look. Naturally light lipsticks give a translucent look and make lips appear naturally reddened—something like biting into a luscious peach and having the juice stain your mouth. (If you have a habit of constantly wetting your lips— DON'T. It not only takes off color, but it leads to chapping and drying.)

Avoid harsh, penciled eyebrows. They give eyes a hard, artificial look. Instead, use a soft, upward stroke with a pencil (or fine point brush) and then powder over lightly and upward to soften. When it comes to eye shadow, it's a soft, subtle look you want; so choose from among delicate pastel tones.

If you wear eyeglasses, apply your makeup as though you didn't wear eyeglasses. Never apply eye makeup to complement your glasses. However, if the lenses of your glasses are heavily magnified, do go somewhat lighter on the total amount of eye makeup you use.

I think a mature woman whose face is totally devoid of lines looks unnatural, often downright eerie. Still, there are lines...and then there are *lines*. There are "smile lines," for instance, that start at the corners of your nose and stem down to the corners of your mouth. If they're only lightly placed, they can look quite charming, expressive, friendly. But if they're really deep, they're aging. Often they give you a haggard, unpleasant look. Well here's what makeup can do about them and a few other problems that get in the way of your looking and feeling 29 Forever.

"Smile Lines" Here is where your highlight goes to work. With the tip of a finger or the corner of a sponge, place a small amount of highlight in the crease of your smile line. Then with finger or

sponge, gently rub up and down until it's perfectly blended and the offensive smile line is practically nonexistent.

Double Chin Apply a darker foundation—about two or three shades darker than your base—directly under the chin and over the heavy area. Blend it upward from the neck to the jawline.

Puffs above Eyelids Place your darker than usual foundation on this area and a light eye shadow on the upper lids and just above your brow, all of which will put the emphasis on the upper lids, and puffs will appear to recede.

Puffs or Bags under Eyes Use your foundation over the area, and then your highlight on the rim just under the puffs or bags. Then blend the colors together gently to avoid any harsh line of demarcation.

Dark Shadows under Eyes Blot your makeup sponge on a tissue to remove any excess base foundation. Apply the smallest amount of highlight and blend carefully from the inner corners of your eyes over the area of your dark shadows. Blotting and using your foundation sponge will erase the starkness of the highlight. Gently blend over the lines of demarcation.

Thin Lips Outline your mouth with a darker shade of lipstick (or, using a light touch, a soft brown eyebrow pencil) just outside the natural edge of the lips. Don't be obvious. Usually the slightest amount of correction will do. Make certain one color "fades" into the other. For an even more luscious look, add—delicately—a white or beige lipstick to the center of your lips.

Droopy Mouth Corners Put your highlight in the crease lines just outside the lower corners of your mouth. Then put a shade darker than your regular lipstick within all four corner edges. Be sure to stop *before* the lipline turns downward. The idea, you see, is to de-emphasize the droop by applying the darker shade to these negative-looking corners.

After you've worked your makeup magic, don't overlook one last important step. Be sure to check it out from different angles and not just headon. Use a hand mirror or, even better, a three-way mirror.

7

The Body Beautiful

SINCE BEAUTY IS in the eye of the beholder (and that also includes *you* staring at *you* in your mirror), who's to say which body is the Body Beautiful?

There are those who consider the fragile bones and boyish lines of a Mia Farrow to be divinely feminine. Others, who might consider a body like that too puny to be beautiful, eye the gentle curves of a Bardot and find themselves sighing with envy. And then there are those who would eat pasta every day for breakfast if, instead of merely making them fat, it would give them the lavishly structured body of a Sophia Loren.

Personally I think each type is a beautiful body.

Be perfectly realistic about your body. Recognize the fact that your basic figure type is largely preprogrammed by your genes. But please don't use that as an excuse for a less than beautiful body. Determine instead that, whatever your basic figure type, you will have a *beautiful* body. Don't waste precious time yearning for a long, willowy figure if you stand 5'1" in your stocking feet. Don't waste precious time yearning for a cuddly, petite figure if you are 5'9" and large boned. No amount of stuffing will turn a Farrow-type into a Loren-type, nor will starving reverse the "miracle." Accept your basic figure type and then set about beautifying it.

I suppose we've all passed through a stage when we wished we looked like somebody else. I know I did. I remember as a teenager being a slave to those commercial scales where—for a penny—you got not only your weight on a card but your fortune as well. I was usually delighted with my fortune (they were invariably so upbeat), and miserable with my weight. Oh how I pined for soft, cuddly curves! As if to reinforce my depression, on the great glass-moon face of the scale was printed the "ideal" weight for each height. I'd find mine (that's right, I'd look each time, despite the fact that the "ideal" never varied from scale to scale), and then slouch away humiliated.

Today, of course, we've all grown so much wiser. We know that there is no "ideal" weight for a given height. Ah, but there *is* a guide for "ideal" figure proportions. And this is it: your bust and lower hip should measure *about* the same size; your waist 10 inches smaller. So whether you're the Farrow-type, the Bardot-type, or the Loren-type, that holds true. It's all a matter of proportion.

Take your measurements and see how you measure up. But first things first. *Strip*. To the buff. *Au naturel*.

Then with a flexible tape (which you should hold snugly, but not tightly), take your true measurements in the areas of bust, lower waist, and hips.

When measuring your bust be certain to measure over the *fullest* part and straight across the back.

Measure your *natural* waistline. By that I mean the smallest part. And don't cheat, please. Don't take a deep breath and hold it; it's an awful temptation, but *don't*.

Finally the hips: I know it sounds cruel, but here you must measure at the fullest part, which is about seven inches below the natural waistline on a short figure, and nine inches below on a tall figure.

All done? Now, if your measurements are—in your candid opinion—something less than "ideal," bear this in mind: only diet will shed excess poundage. Exercise will get your body fit and keep it fit. But exercise is not of itself a reducer.

There are literally scads of diets to choose from. There are as many diet books as there are diets. Read as many as you like, but before you start a diet I urge you to check in with your personal physician. A diet, after all, is very personal. Don't be influenced by the new sylphlike figure of a formerly fat friend and her enthusiasm for the diet that worked the miracle. That's *her* diet. You find yours with, I repeat, the help of your personal physician.

Singer Peggy Lee was overweight for years and took to wearing caftans onstage to conceal her *embonpoint*. She says she had given up all hope of ever losing weight. "For years I had tried everything—a hundred diets, spas, an electric bicycle, a roller. Nothing worked. Once I checked into a hospital and told them, 'For God's sake, starve me!' I lived on two hundred and fifty calories a day, and at the end of ten days I had lost a pound and a half. Can you believe that? I could have wept. Then I met this marvelous doctor from the Mayo Clinic. He took all kinds of tests and gave me this special diet. And finally I lost. It's so marvelous to be thin again!"

See what I mean? See your doctor before dieting.

Meanwhile, dieting or not, you should exercise. There is some form of daily exercise that is suitable to your lifestyle, temperament, and physical condition that can fit neatly and comfortably into the stream of your day-to-day pattern.

Some form of exercise is vital if you want a body that's lithe and toned from top to bottom. For no matter how beautifully proportioned your body is, if it doesn't move sensuously and bend freely, it isn't a young body.

The 29 Forever spirit is young and it must have a body to match. There's no room for rigidity. Furthermore, along with a youthfully supple body, the proper exercise will give you firm skin...a glowing complexion...better digestion...more energy...and a glorious allover feeling of well-being. There is a good deal of scientific evidence that physical exertion increases brain power as well. Let's face it—a trim, limber body is certainly a sexy one. Regular exercise will enhance your sex life, too. An active, satisfying sex life is an important part of being 29 Forever.

Having said all that, I have a confession to make. I don't exercise regularly. By that I mean I have no set exercise regimen, as do so many of my friends. I find systematic exercise boring. It just doesn't fit neatly and comfortably into the stream of my day-to-day pattern. This is not so for most of my friends.

As one puts it, "It's very important to me to have a fixed exercise period every day, no matter where I happen to be. It's important mentally and emotionally as well as physically. I like the discipline and I like myself for following it."

Yet when it comes to the form their exercise takes, the every-day exercisers break ranks, which is as it should be. Exercise, like diet, is very personal. You must find a regimen that suits you.

Some women exercise alone in the privacy of their homes. Others take off for an exercise class, preferring the stimulation of group exercise. Still others, who can afford the tab (often as high as $1,000 per week), jet to a beauty spa; while some flip on their television set at home and exercise along with a televised instructor. I know a few models who, when on a location job, carry with them cassettes of recorded exercises.

Some women prefer exercise that has the added allure of a philosophy about it, Yoga, for instance, while others opt for something more strenuous and less cerebral.

Well, my plan is really no plan. But that doesn't mean that I don't keep a watchful eye on my figure. I do. I like to believe that I can "feel" it if my waistline expands so much as a fraction of an inch, or when my hips even threaten to spread. But of course I don't actually rely on my feelings to let me know when I'm in danger. I look to my bathroom scale and my tape measure. You mustn't depend on your bathroom scale alone, since your figure can spread without your gaining so much as half a pound.

What do I do when I find my proportions sliding *out of proportion?* I spot-exercise. If it's my hips that are misbehaving, for example, then it's on my hips I concentrate. For as long as it takes to bring them back into line, I'm every bit as systematic and fanatical about my exercising as any of my everyday exercise friends.

I don't suggest that everyone should follow my example. It suits me. It may not suit you. I find that I don't need a fixed exercise regimen. I'm an extremely active person. I walk a *minimum* of one mile a day, sometimes three. When I'm not walking, I'm riding a bicycle or jumping rope. In season I swim, ride horseback, play a little tennis or golf, and ski; all of which helps keep my figure fit.

So when I urge you to exercise to get fit and stay fit, whatever you choose to do should please you, make you happy. Exercise should never be a chore; it should be fun. It should be approached with a joyful attitude. Perhaps if more people saw it in that light, more people would exercise. A recent study made for the President's Council on Fitness showed that approximately 45 percent of American adults don't exercise at all.

Smart women do, of course. They do whatever exercises give them the most pleasure and, since this keeps them at it, it never fails to produce the desired results. Certainly that was the message that came across from a survey conducted by the newspaper *W*.

Dina Merrill, the cool, blonde actress-socialite-businesswoman, said she disdains a regular exercise program. She finds she doesn't need it since, when she's at home on the West Coast, she's constantly playing tennis and golf; and when she's at home on the East Coast, she walks briskly almost everywhere she goes.

Then we have Deborah Kerr, with red-gold hair and a fabulous complexion. She does ten minutes of situps in the morning, every morning. When she happens to be in California, she follows up with a swim. "A dip in the ocean revives me like nothing else."

Cosmetic queen Estée Lauder swims every day when she's at her home in Palm Beach or her villa on the Côte d'Azur, and plays tennis three or four times a week.

Mala Rubinstein, another cosmetic queen, confides that exercise is a daily word with her. "If I go from the bedroom to the bathroom, I'll stretch up and walk on my toes. I do bicycle exercises on the bed, especially after standing on my feet all day. And I walk whenever I can."

Rose Kennedy has no regular exercise regimen other than the fact that "I walk three or four miles a day." Although I understand that, when she's in Hyannisport in summer and Palm Beach in winter, she swims daily and plays golf several times a week.

Says the amazingly youthful Merle Oberon: "I've done Yoga and swimming practically every day of my life."

"Swim whenever you can," physical therapist Manya Kahn urges her fashionable clients. "It's one of the best exercises because your whole body is on a level plane and every muscle is in action."

Gloria Swanson rides a stationary bicycle every day in her bedroom. Recently in Hollywood, where she finished still another film, she asked for an upstairs dressing room just for the exercise of running up and down.

Joanne Woodward exercises and dances five mornings a week at a ballet school to avoid being what she calls "a middle-aged slunk." She started the lessons at age thirty-five—eight years ago—when she admitted she was getting flabby.

Cristina Ford, the Italian-born beauty, walks two hours a day, "come rain or shine."

And Betty Ford, who was once a professional dancer, told *W* she normally devotes at least fifteen minutes a day to modern-dance exercise. It works, too. She's 5'6" and weighs 108 pounds.

So you see, there are many, many ways to stay fit. In answer to the question *What is an ideal fitness schedule?,* Dr. Warren R. Guild, a leading sports and medicine authority, replies, "one basic enjoyable sport that is pretty much possible the year 'round as the main course, plus seasonal sports as dessert. This means a person can be in shape twelve months of the year."

Taking that thought a step further, Dr. Guild says he regards swimming, jogging, bicycling, and tennis as probably the best sports for overall fitness. They're what I call the lifelong sports. If you must confine your energies to just one of them, I say make it swimming, since that calls into action *every* part of your body.

You say you're not the sporting type? Then WALK. It's a sensible, year-round exercise for which you don't need special equipment other than your own pair of legs. Your leg muscles act as a circulation pump, working to get blood back to your heart. But if walking is to do you good, you must walk *briskly* and *erect*.

When Rose Kennedy does her three or four miles a day, you can be certain it's a brisk walk. I've seen her covering ground in Central Park, so I know. According to a niece of hers, "If you kept up with her, it would be better than spending a week at a beauty spa." And her posture is *perfect*.

Picking up the pace of your walk is easy. But improving your posture isn't, since it means undoing some practically lifelong habits. Poor posture is figure sabotage. Poor standing posture breeds a double chin, dowager's hump, pot belly, and sway back. (Your proportions may be perfection, but with one or more of those figure "blemishes," who'd care?) Poor sitting posture (some women who stand erect forget all about good posture when they sit) adds to that awful list the so-called *stenographer's spread*.

The damage isn't confined to your figure. "When you slump," says Dr. Charles L. Lowman, who was named "Doctor of the Century" by the Los Angeles Medical Society, "the heart lies sideways and it has to work harder from that position. Your blood circulation is poorer too when you slump, which puts even more strain on the heart.

"Habitual slumping can also cause varicose veins, infection in the colon, kidney disease, pinched nerves leading to painful disorders such as sciatica, and more wear and tear all over your body, causing you to age faster."

And Dr. Lowman practices what he preaches. At ninety-four, he stands tall (6′2″) and erect as a cavalry officer. Superb health, he maintains, just isn't possible without good posture. According to Dr. Lowman, about 75 percent of American youths have bad posture.

In the words of Marjorie Craig, who is in charge of exercise at Elizabeth Arden: "Even if your measurements are down to where they should be, if you stand wrong, you'll look ten pounds heavier and, of course, older."

As one who slouched her way through her early teens, I am—like any reformed sinner—full of fire and brimstone when it comes to good posture. Good posture means putting your body in alignment, which is another way of saying, learn to stand in balance and everything will fall into proper place. That's what good posture is all about: flat tummy, straight back, buttocks tucked under.

Here is how to put your body in alignment—a kind of balancing act from the bottom up:

• Stand with your feet a few inches apart, toes pointing straight ahead and arms hanging loosely at your sides.

• Distribute your weight evenly on both legs by pressing on the ball of each foot. Tighten the muscles in the front of your thighs.

• Slowly draw the buttocks tightly together.

• Next, slowly stretch your spine and draw your shoulder blades together, but take care not to lift your shoulders or tilt your chin in the doing.

Start each day by putting your body in alignment this way, until good posture is finally natural with you. "Make a conscious effort at first," says Dr. Lowman, "and soon good posture habits will come automatically."

Sometimes one of the legacies of poor posture is the dowager's hump at the base of the neck. Proper posture will eventually chase it away once and for all, but to hasten its exit, I suggest the following exercise:

Lie flat on your back on the floor, knees straight, toes pointed and arms at sides. Breathe in slowly as you raise head and knees (shoulders remain on floor); and clasping knees with both hands, bend your knees to your chest. Hold this position to the count of three. Then, breathing out, return to starting position. Do a total of five repetitions.

Here's an exercise specially designed to ease you into the habit of good posture:

1) Lie flat on your back on the floor, knees straight, hands on hips. Breathing in, raise both legs about ten inches off the floor. Hold to the slow count of two.

2) Breathing out, lower legs to the floor. Breathing in, raise both legs ten inches again.

3) Now, raise right leg still another ten inches. Hold to slow count of 2. Breathing out, lower it to the level of your left leg. Repeat exercise with left leg, breathing rhythmically.

My Own Exercise Plan

As I've already told you, I don't exercise faithfully every day. But when I do, I'm a fanatic about it. Here are my exercises, and I can tell you that they work wonders.

For the Bosom

We have two muscles *under* the breast tissue. (Your breasts are all tissue, not a single muscle.) My friend Dr. Jerry Rosenblatt (Chief of Surgery at LeRoy Hospital in New York) says, "The proper exercise of these two muscles can help prevent sagging breasts, as it's these pectoral muscles that hold the tissues up." Diet, too, plays an important part. The proper diet nourishes the tissue, producing healthy cells which, in turn, build healthy tissue. Healthy breast tissue is usually firmer.

Remember: it's not the size of your breasts that counts. What counts is the firmness of contour. Now on to our exercises.

1) Try to touch your elbows behind your back several times each day.

2) Hold your shoulders back, arms spread-eagle, and breathe deeply. Now with both arms simultaneously, make complete circles about six inches in diameter.

3) Lock both hands behind your head with elbows at ear level. Push forward with entire upper body as though you were trying to send your head rolling. Hold push to a count of ten.

4)   Stand or, if you prefer, sit. Grab your left elbow with your right hand, and your right elbow with your left hand. Then push elbows against each hand as if you were trying to separate the arms.

5)   Lock hands and hold in front above your waist. Push with your palms against each other in a hard, fast motion so that you feel your arms jerked downward.

6)   Standing, clasp your hands in front of you at eye level. Squeeze hands. Then swing them around to the back and clasp again as high as you possibly can, straightening the arms.

7)   Pushups are great for firming those all-important pectoral muscles. Lie flat on the floor with your face down, arms bent at sides (hands at shoulder level) for support. Now raise your body, taking care to have your weight distributed evenly between your hands and feet. Lower again. Don't overdo. Six repetitions are enough.

8)   Lie flat on your back on the bed. Hold both arms out straight. Move them in a rapid zigzag motion, each arm crossing the other's path. It is important that you keep arms STRAIGHT throughout this exercise. Do ten repetitions.

For the Waist

1)   Stand with your feet about eighteen inches apart, and arms held horizontal at shoulder level. Swing from the waist as far to the right as possible, turning your head to follow the arm that is moving backward. Push that arm as far back as it can go without moving your feet. Return to starting

position and repeat, this time swing as far to the left as possible. Do six repetitions.

2) Stand with feet about eighteen inches apart, your back and knees straight. Raise both arms straight up over your head. Very slowly bend back both hands at the wrists until palms face the ceiling. Then slowly stretch as though you really believed you could touch the ceiling. S-t-r-e-t-c-h as far as you can without rising off the floor and hold to the count of six. Then bring your arms down to your, sides and start over again. Six repetitions are enough.

3) Lie flat on your back on the floor, with arms and legs outstretched. Sit up without changing the position of arms and legs. Now bend to touch your left foot with fingertips of both hands, meanwhile keeping your head bent low. Repeat on your right side. Do six repetitions.

4) Lie flat on your back on the floor, but this time with feet together and arms at your sides. Raise your left leg high as possible while keeping your knees straight. Try to touch toes of your left leg with your right hand. Return to starting position and repeat with right leg and left hand. Six repetitions will do.

For Upper Arms

Swimming's excellent for the upper arms, which lose muscle tone early. Tennis is great, too. So, I might add, is using your vacuum cleaner, with all that arm action involved when poking it into corners and under furniture. Super-great are these arm-firming exercises.

1)   Stand erect with both arms at your sides. Make tight fists and slowly bring both arms backwards and up as far as they can go. Hold to the count of six and bring arms slowly down and back to starting position. Stay fisted and repeat for a total of ten repetitions.

2)   Stand erect, this time with both arms extended forward at shoulder level. Keep arms perfectly straight, but stretch the right arm six times, as though you were reaching for something. Return to starting position and stretch left arm six times. For each arm do a total of six repetitions.

3)   Lie on the floor—perfectly straight—on your left side with both feet touching the floor. Grasping your neck with your right hand for balance, push yourself off the floor with your left arm and left leg. Then slowly lower yourself back to the floor. Repeat six times on the left side and then turn to your right side and repeat six more times.

4)   (This one's splendid for firming the backs of your arms.) Stand on the floor by the foot of your bed. With your back to the bed, slowly squat until buttocks are at a level with the bed. Then brace both hands on the foot of the bed and "sit" on nothing. From this "precarious" perch, lower buttocks to the floor, then rise to position where buttocks are "sitting" on nothing again and repeat descent to the floor. Go up and down six times and never, never raise heels off the floor at any point.

For Your Stomach

I was almost tempted to say *tummy* and decided against it. Why mince words? It's your stomach we're concerned with, and there's simply no way to reduce it by applying a cuddly sounding diminutive like *tummy*.

Recently I attended a performance of a play starring a film actress whose figure looked lovely, until she turned profile and one caught sight of her bulging stomach. I had everything I could do not to drop backstage after the final curtain with these exercises scribbled for her benefit on the back of my program.

1) (This one's so subtle that you can do it anytime, anywhere.) Stand straight, with feet together and both hands at your sides. Inhale slowly as you also very slowly tighten your stomach muscles. Keep it up until you are almost convinced that, yes, you actually have those stomach muscles pushing up against your spinal column. When you have, hold to the count of ten and release slowly. Do this stomach lift for six repetitions. And do it several times a day.

2) Lie flat on the floor on your back, feet together and arms at your sides, palms down. Slowly raise both legs up off the floor, and then quickly pull them to a bent-knee position. Hold to the slow count of three, then straighten both legs and slowly raise them until toes are pointing straight at the ceiling. S-l-o-w-l-y lower legs simultaneously, allowing them to almost reach the floor, at which point (about two inches from the floor) you will suddenly pull them back to your bent-knee position. Return to starting position. Do four repetitions.

3) Lie flat on the floor on your back, with feet together and arms at your sides, palms down. Slowly raise your feet about four inches off the

floor—no more than four inches, please—while simultaneously raising your head just high enough to give you a peek at those rising toes. Holding that position, start to climb, hand-over-hand fashion, a makebelieve rope to the count of twenty. Return to starting position. Do five repetitions.

4) Lie flat on the floor on your back, arms straight back and palms facing the ceiling. Relax. Then sit up quickly, swinging your arms forward and jackknifing your knees to your chest all in one swift motion, keeping elbows stiff and toes pointed. Return to starting position. This isn't an easy exercise, so start with only two repetitions and gradually work up to six.

For Your Hips

Hips, Hips Away! What more can I say? except that when I think HIPS, I inevitably think, too, of that old song that goes, "...the hip bone's connected to the thigh bone...the thigh bone's connected to the..." Why? because the following exercises not only attend to your hips, but firm thighs, too.

1) Kneel on your knees. Bend forward and place both palms flat on the floor. Now bring your left leg to the side, while keeping your knee stiff and toes pointed. Next, rapidly raise and lower that leg. Do twelve repetitions with left leg, and then twelve with right leg.

2) Lie flat on your back, with feet together and arms extended at shoulder level. Keeping knees stiff and toes pointed, lift your left leg straight up until toes point directly toward the ceiling. Swing left leg

over your right leg, until left leg touches the floor. Return to starting position and repeat with right leg. Do ten repetitions.

3) Roll over and lie face down on the floor, with elbows out at shoulder level, and hands supporting your chin. Raise your left leg, keeping knee stiff and toes pointed. Stretch leg up and back as far as possible. Hold leg up for count of six and then return leg to starting position on the floor. Repeat with right leg. Do six repetitions for each leg.

For Buttocks

Some women are so appalled at the sight of their sagging buttocks that they get themselves off to a plastic surgeon and get a derrière lift. I maintain that a slimming diet and proper exercise will keep buttocks firm and, as an added bonus, these exercises that firm the behind will also improve the appearance of the outside thighs.

1) Kneel on your knees, arms straight, palms down. Look straight ahead. Lift left leg, keeping it bent, raise your knee and lower your head until they meet. Now slowly straighten, arching your back and swinging left leg back and up as far as it will go. Hold this position for count of five. Return to starting position and repeat with right leg. Do six repetitions for both legs.

2) Kneel and grasp the side of a chair or couch with both hands. Protrude derrière as far back as possible without your knees moving off the floor. Push pelvis in toward chair or couch. Next, raise your left leg to the back as high as you can without

pulling pelvis out of tuck position. Relax pelvis. Rest. Repeat exercise, this time raising right leg. Do six repetitions for both legs.

3) Lie face down on the floor, chin outstretched, arms at sides. Lift left leg as high as possible, while keeping pelvis flat—in short, the reverse action of the preceding exercise. Hold and then lower. Now lift *both* legs together. Press down with fists, keeping your knees straight. Hold, lower. Repeat exercise, this time lifting right leg and then both legs. Do six repetitions.

4) Lie face down at the foot of your bed. In other words, your stomach is on the bed but your legs are extended beyond the bed. Take a firm hold of the mattress sides with both hands. Raise each leg alternately to horizontal position. Repeat ten times for each leg.

5) (This exercise is extremely effective in tightening stomach muscles, along with buttocks.) Sit at a table or desk in a straightback chair, shoes off. Place hands on the edge of the table or desk and push hard against it, tightening buttock muscles while you lift your legs until they're extended out straight and parallel with the floor. Now point your toes and hold this position to the count of six. Then flex your toes five times. Relax and return to starting position. Do six repetitions.

One Perfect Exercise

Is it possible there is one *exercise that tones every muscle of the body? There is:*

1)   Start out lying flat on the floor, face down, with arms bent at elbows as though you were planning to do pushups.

2)   Straighten your arms and slowly lift your torso off the floor.

3)   Keeping your spine level and stomach taut, start slipping back—disc by disc—until you're sitting on your heels.

4)   Then very s-l-o-w-l-y do all your body work in reverse until you are back in your first position.

Is Going Braless for You?

It is for me. On occasion. It depends on any number of variables. There are times when I enjoy feeling completely free, and looking natural and bouncy. Other times I'd rather be less distracting, when I'm feeling less extroverted, more serious and contemplative.

Like everything else in life, to wear a bra or not is very individual. I would suggest, however, that you avoid going braless during the few days just prior to your cycle, because that's when breasts are fullest and heaviest. That's when you very definitely need the support of a bra, or you invite sagging.

If you think you're too small or too large to go braless, but you want to try the look, I suggest you use this surgical tape trick: cut a length of surgical adhesive tape (either the 1″ or 1½″ width) long enough to reach from under your arm to the center of your bosom. Then stick the tape down at underarm and press around under your breasts, lifting them and using the tape for support.

A Few Well-Chosen Words
about Nipples

The nipple is the only truly *erotic* part of the breast. Consequently, who (who, indeed!) tolerates even the wispiest wisp of hair around the nipples? Ask your doctor about the safest removal method. Hair between the breasts? that's simpler to remove. Waxing is usually recommended.

Icy-cold water has a lively effect on nipples. It firms the breasts and emphasizes the nipples. Try a splash of icy-cold water after a shower. You might also rub your breasts gently with an ice cube, when you're planning to go braless. Oldtime movie siren Jean Harlow never wore a bra and, just before sweeping into camera range, she would apply ice to her breasts. See one of her old flicks and you'll see the result even through a satin sheath!

Rouge your nipples? You might. But I put that in

the same class with rouging knees. (I've done both, but not often.) Still, a subtle bit of bosom makeup can do a lot to suggest a gleaming, swelling bosom when it's not quite so gleaming and swelling. Here's how: apply a darkish shade of blusher (powder form) in the hollow between your breasts. Next, blend a pearly off-white highlighter (powder or nongreasy liquid) on the top slope of each breast. Then add a generous dab of perfume between your breasts. With all that, who needs rouged nipples?

8

Those Fabulous Extremities: Feet and Legs

THE BODY BEAUTIFUL includes thighs...kneecaps ...toes. Most women are thigh conscious...only half-aware of kneecaps...and indifferent about toes until theirs hurt. Well let's begin at the bottom, with your feet—very likely the most neglected part of your body.

Certainly feet are hard workers, and all too often treated like drudges. They're stuffed into shoes that are too tight, too small; so rarely creamed, if at all; scented seldom, if ever. Oh, but they do get their revenge. Sore, unhappy feet can give you wrinkles! (It's not for nothing that it's often said we wear our shoes on our face.) Sore, unhappy feet can sabotage that perfect posture you've worked so hard to attain!

Why let your feet damage your good looks when, with the proper attention, they can be happy, pretty feet? Troubled feet certainly aren't young feet.

For youthful, pretty feet—feet free of calluses, corns, and blemishes; feet that look and feel satiny smooth—you need a small but mighty arsenal of beauty aids: a camphored cream for massaging; a cooling talcum powder; a box of tissues; a toenail clipper and file; a pumice stone; and polish. That's what you need for the super every-ten-day beauty treatment your feet so rightly deserve.

1) Begin by slipping those tired feet of yours into soothingly warm, soapy water. Let them soak. Sit and relax. Then start massaging the soapy water into the skin.

2) Next, using the pumice stone, smooth the skin on the backs of your heels and the bottoms of your feet.

3) Towel dry and, with your toenail clipper, clip nails almost straight across, just slightly below the tip of the toe. (Ingrown nails come as a result of cutting away the sides of the nails.)

4) File your nails smooth.

5) Push cuticles back with a cotton-wrapped orange stick.

6) Now comes the most satisfying part of the beauty treatment as far as I'm concerned: massaging with a rich, camphored cream. Really knead it into the feet. It's so cooling, so refreshing! Don't rush. Massage. Massage. Massage until your feet tingle with pleasure.

7) Scrub toenails with a good bristle brush to remove any residue of cream.

8) Puff dry and scent with the cooling talcum powder.

9) Now you're ready for your pedicure. Pluck some tissue out of the box and twist strips of it between each toe to keep polish from smudging. Apply a base coat for protection, then two coats of color.

Those Fabulous Extremities: Feet and Legs
A Potpourri of Tips for Youthful,
Pretty Feet

... To relax tired feet, elevate them during the day and sleep at night with a pillow under your knees. Treat them to alternating hot and cold foot baths.

... Go barefoot as often as possible, indoors and outdoors. What a relief! Walking barefoot on a surface such as sand or grass, which has some "give" to it, is a super foot exercise. Feet react to the soothing touch of fresh air, and how they delight in a walk through cooling water. Walking in the lapping surf is a marvelous exercise for your legs, and the sand acts like a very gentle pumice to the soles of your feet.

... Swollen feet (often commonplace during the hot summer months)? Try a foot bath containing Epsom salts.

... Perspiring feet? Splash on witch hazel that's been cooled in your refrigerator.

... If the skin of your heels seems determined to stay dingy looking despite all your soaking, rub them with a paste made of cleansing grains mixed with water.

... Too tight hosiery? Like too tight shoes, they're damaging to your feet; can actually encourage ingrown toenails. Get rid of them! Stockings should extend a half-inch beyond your longest toe.

... Always buy your shoes late in the afternoon, when your feet are their maximum size and therefore most sensitive to fit. (Difference from morning to late afternoon, for example, can be as much as one whole size.) Your shoes should be ¾" to 1" longer than your longest toe.

Change shoes often. Alternate heavy shoes with flimsy little sandals. Allow your feet *freedom*.

... Protect your feet from calluses. That's so much more sensible than waiting till they appear and then getting rid of them. Here's what to do: soak your feet in a solution of fluffy tannic-acid powder and warm water for a period of about ten minutes. It will work as a kind of invisible shield against calluses.

Exercises for Youthful, Pretty Feet

Courtesy of the New York State College of Home Economics, Cornell University. They're recommended for troublefree feet; that is, feet with no serious problems. Still, I wouldn't suggest you start out doing each one the maximum number of times. Start instead with one-third the number of repetitions mentioned for each exercise, and then build up gradually. No strain that way. *Reward:* youthful, shapely feet.

1) *For ankles and arches.* Standing with your feet parallel (six to eight inches apart) go up on your tiptoes and return slowly, counting to ten. This exercises the strong leg muscles and strengthens the foot muscles, which, in turn, helps relieve the rigidity of the ankles and long arch. Do five to ten repetitions.

2) *For arches*. Stand with feet parallel (about six inches apart). Rise up on your toes, roll feet outward and back onto heel about fifteen to twenty times so that your weight comes on the outside border of your feet. Lift inner and under parts of the feet clear off the floor at each roll. It helps relieve the strain of the inner arch, and tones up the muscles of the outer arch.

3) *For ankles*. Sit on a chair with your right leg over your left knee. Bend your right foot down, in toward ankle, and up. Repeat ten to fifteen times. Reverse direction of circle for ten to fifteen times. Then put left leg over right knee and repeat the same motions with the left foot. This helps relieve stiffness of the ankle-arch joint.

4) *For toes*. Sit in a relaxed position. Try to pick up a towel, marble, or pencil by grasping with your toes. This exercise keeps your toes agile and strengthens the arch across the ball of the foot. Do ten to fifteen repetitions.

5) *For calf to heel*. Sit on the floor with legs straight ahead. Bend your feet upward as far as you can. This strengthens the calf of the leg and heel muscles. Repeat ten to fifteen times.

6) *For balance muscles*. Stand stiff kneed, with legs crossed, feet parallel (three or four inches apart—weight should be divided evenly between both feet). Hold this position for one minute. Reverse. This superb exercise actually brings into use every muscle of balance; helps put a gloss on your now-perfect posture so that when you walk you almost seem to float! Do ten to fifteen repetitions.

7) *For arch and leg muscles*. Sit on the floor

with your legs straight ahead. Turn the bottoms of the feet closely together. *Don't* bend the knees. Repeat ten times.

8) *For toes and feet.* Stand with feet parallel and bend toes upward as far as possible and return to the floor slowly. Do ten to fifteen repetitions.

Some women thank the Good Lord for the fashion acceptance of pants. They're that grateful for a chance to hide their legs! Pity, when youthful, pretty legs are so downright alluring; plus the happy fact that a woman's legs are so durable that often when her figure sags, her legs still retain their youthful prettiness. Even when neglected, legs respond to loving care quickly.

Scrupulous skin care and exercise—that's the winning ticket for legs that are lissome, satiny smooth, and gracefully curved.

Who needs fuzzy legs? Certainly no beauty-conscious woman with a 29 Forever spirit! So off with the fuzz for a sleek, hairfree look and feel. Choose the method you feel most comfortable with: shaving, depilatory, or waxing.

Shaving is not recommended for a long-lasting effect, because it cuts the hair off at exactly the skin-surface level. Meanwhile hair continues to grow at its root. Still, it's fast and relatively simple today, what with electric razors perfected to the point of barely leaving a visible root. Twin-blade injector razors are very light and easy to handle, and they rarely nick when you slather on one of the For-Women-Only shaving creams.

Depilatory, in the form of a cream or lotion, softens and weakens the hair shafts, with the result that the hair can be wiped right off the legs after a brief waiting time. A depilatory will leave your legs smoother and softer than shaving, but the effect is not as long-lasting as that of waxing. Scented sprayon depilatories are, I think, the easiest since all you have to do is press the button, wait about five minutes, and then rinse or shower away the unwanted hair.

Waxing is the method favored at most beauty salons. Of course, you may purchase waxes yourself at any cosmetic counter. Waxing gives the longest-lasting results. Some waxes you can buy must be warmed first and then allowed to cool on your skin, while others are ready to go to work as soon as you open the package and apply. Waxing is perfectly safe and, contrary to some rumors, it doesn't cause any increased coarseness of the hairs.

A Potpourri of Tips for Youthful, Pretty Legs

Tiny blemishes? surface veins? and even your panty hose can't completely conceal them? Use leg makeup. But be sure to blend it well if you want no silly streaks marring the smooth, flawless look leg makeup can give when carefully applied.

To prevent varicose veins, *walk briskly*—and a lot. Walking causes your leg muscles to contract, thus improving the circulation in your legs.

Water-softened hair is easiest to remove if you use a safety razor. I suggest you shave your legs while soaking in the tub. If you use an electric razor (naturally you don't use it in the tub), try a preshave lotion to reduce the razor's pull.

Want to give your knees a super polish? Rub them with a paste made of cleansing grains mixed with water. A good scrub with it will also remove dry, flaky skin.

Legs too heavy? Avoid bulky textured hose. Of course, dark shades are the most slimming. Plain pumps are best; avoid thin straps and flats.

Legs too thin? Avoid stockings that are too dark. Invest in warm, lively shades; the lighter the shade, the heavier your leg will appear. When it comes to footwear, choose a medium-low heel, but certainly avoid a clumpy-type shoe. A too high heel makes thin legs look thinner.

For that satiny-smooth look and feel, add bath oil to your tub and give your legs a daily massage with a rich cream or lotion, working in an extra amount at your knees and heels to prevent thickened skin and roughness.

Exercises for Youthful, Pretty Legs

For shapelier calves and ankles.

1) Stand about four feet away and place your palms flat on a wall. Turn your toes inward and roll the weight of your body onto the outer edges of your feet.

2) Lie flat on your back on your bed with heels against the wall. Grasp the sides of the mattress

firmly with your hands, then push away from the wall. Use your toes—not your heels—while, at the same time, pulling back with your hands.

3) Rise on your toes and walk around the room. Then walk in reverse. Next, walk sideways, bringing one leg across the other.

4) Standing up straight, bring your hands together in a prayerlike position with fingers pointing upward. Now flex your left leg by placing the sole of your foot firmly against your right thigh. Breathe deeply to the slow count of six. Exhale. Relax and repeat exercise, this time flexing right leg and bringing foot firmly against your left thigh.

For shapelier knees.

1) Kneel with your legs flat against the floor. Taking a deep breath, arch your torso backwards and grasp your ankles with your hands. Hold. Exhale. Return to starting position. Relax about three seconds and repeat exercise.

2) Pull a straight-back chair up before a table. Place both legs straight out under the table, with your toes touching the underside of the table. Next, press both feet upward, as though you planned to actually lift the table off the floor. Hold that position to the count of six. Relax three seconds and repeat exercise.

For slimmer thighs.

1) Kneel on all fours. Extend your left leg straight out to the side and bounce it up and down,

keeping the rest of your body motionless and as straight as possible. Return to starting position and repeat exercise with right leg. (This one's a dandy for your outside thighs.)

2)   Lie on your right side, resting your weight on your right upper arm. Raise your left leg straight up, pointing toes toward the ceiling. Flex your ankle—up, down, up, down. Your inner thigh muscles will tighten as your ankle flexes.

3)   Sit on the floor with your knees wide apart, soles of your feet together, and hands pressed against inside knees. Take a deep breath and bend torso forward, toward your feet. Hold to the count of six, while you exhale, inhale, exhale, inhale. Straighten up to assume starting position. Exhale.

4)   Sit on the floor with your knees wide apart, soles of your feet together, and bring your hands together in a prayerlike position with fingers pointing upward, elbows pressed against inside thighs. Push your legs together while using your arms to resist the push. Hold legs together to the count of six. Relax about three seconds and do this exercise in reverse; that is, use your elbows to force your thighs outward. Again, hold this position to the count of six. Relax three seconds and repeat exercise.

5)   Stand erect, hands on hips, feet about ten inches apart. Take a deep breath and lower to a squatting position, raising both heels off the floor and taking care to keep your back straight. Breathing out, return to starting position.

9

Hands Up!

THAT'S RIGHT, up—up where we can see them.

It's *Hand Inspection Time*.

Be perfectly frank. Are they all you could wish for? And your wish should be for soft, alluring, sensuous-looking hands. Settle for nothing less. So if yours are anything less, now's the time to do something about it. Don't be like some of the professional beauties who pampered face and figure, and neglected their hands, spending their days hiding them in tidy white gloves. *Preventive* measures are called for. Once your hands really age—well, there isn't very much you can do about it other than take to wearing those tidy white gloves year 'round.

Be aware that your hands do have a life of their own. For instance, it is possible to have an oily complexion and dry, very dry, hands. What doesn't harm your skin elsewhere may play havoc with the skin of your hands. Exposure to certain detergents, home shampoos, and hair dyes may irritate the skin of your hands. Obviously they should be avoided, unless you wear protective gloves.

Pamper Your Hands

• Avoid very hot or very cold water, and please don't overdo the hand-washing bit. Too frequent washing takes protein out of your nails as well as drying out your hands.

• Use fabric-lined gloves when washing dishes, or when your hands simply must come into contact with a detergent or anything else that you know acts as an irritant to the skin.

• Each time you wash your hands, apply a rich hand cream or lotion. (You might want to look into one that's made from the natural oils of a fresh fruit or vegetable—say, a peach or avocado.) Old-fashioned glycerine and rosewater is still a Grade-A hand lotion, and it's simple to mix your own. Combine two tablespoons of witch hazel...2 tablespoons of glycerine...½ teaspoon of rose soluble oil...and ¼ cup of water. Simply shake together in a bottle, adding the water at the end.

Before applying your hand cream or lotion, be sure to blot hands dry first. Work in cream or lotion with a light circular motion, paying special attention to your knuckles and skin between your fingers. Massage up clear past your wrists. Use your towel to push back cuticles.

• Always remove your ring(s) when your hands

are going to be exposed to soapy water, or when slipping on rubber gloves. Soap and detergents collect under rings and can cause skin irritation.

• Rub a little soap under your nails when you do your gardening chores to prevent soil from "nesting" under your nails.

• Use lemon juice to remove stains from hands and nails.

• Use a pencil or telephone dialer to dial your telephone.

• Broken nails? chipped nails? in other words...DAMAGED nails? If the answer's yes, and you're fortunate enough to have a nail care specialist nearby—someone like Margaret Din of "Margaret," who is here in New York—don't walk, *rush* there. Let her rebuild your nails via "pattinails" that will protect them while they are growing back normal and healthy. Meanwhile nobody, but nobody, will be able to guess the trouble they've seen. (And the "pattinails" look so natural that you can go without nail polish if you want to.)

• Brown spots? Don't feel you must do as some mature beauties of the past have done and "imprison" your hands forever in a pair of gloves. Bleach them out with a mixture of salt and lemon juice.

• Rough, red hands? I call them old-fashioned hands. There's no earthly excuse for hands like that. But if you have allowed yours to get in shocking condition, here's how to get them smooth and fair:

• Soak them in warm (not hot) water for a few minutes.

• Blot dry and slather them with a coating of soothing Vaseline, or A&D ointment, that you can buy at any drugstore. Tissue off the excess.

• Use a rich cream or lotion every time you wash your hands, and carry a minisized jar or bottle of cream or lotion in your handbag.

Exercises for Alluring, Sensuous-Looking Hands

Your hands can be beautiful to look at if they're soft and smooth, but they can't be sensuous looking if they aren't graceful and expressive; any more than a beautiful woman can be interesting if she just sits there, strikes a pose, but never speaks. You want hands with nimble wrists and flexible fingers, hands with a language all their own. These simple hand exercises will help you get them.

1) Make a fist. Hold it to the slow count of 6 and then open your hand fast, spreading your fingers wide apart.

2) Another variation of this exercise: put your hands in your lap, plams down. Spread fingers open slowly—very slowly—as far as you can get them. Hold to the slow count of six and then close them *fast*.

3) Take a rubber ball and squeeze it hard as you can.

4) Hands Up! Literally—it's a nonexercise exercise. Here's how it goes: lean on your elbows and keep your hands up when you're relaxing. Not only will your hands look more graceful that way, but this position will also make the veins in your

hands less noticeable. Remember: hands, like every other part of your body, are fighting the downward pull of gravity. So it should be "Hands Up!" every chance you get.

If you want my nomination for the most alluring, expressive, sensuous-looking hands—they're Barbra Streisand's. In fact, expressive is too pale an adjective. *Eloquent* is more like it.

10

Hair: Nature's Miracle Fiber

EVERY BUSY MODEL is something of a hair expert. She has to be, for often she has to submit to as many as half a dozen changes of hairstyle in a single day—dramatic changes, too. So her poor hair is fair game for an army of hot rollers (sometimes curling irons), fast combings, and blasts of hair spray, none of which are exactly good for the health of her hair. So she'd better know something about hair care or she'll be out of business—and out of hair!

No wonder many models have regular hair checkups. They take themselves off to a hair care specialist who snips a strand of hair . . . puts it under an electron microscope that magnifies it 200 times and takes a professional look at the condition of the hair shaft, root, and cuticle . . . and decides on what treatment, if any, is needed.

If you ever had a look at a magnified strand of damaged hair, you'd beware of teasing, hard combing, and sleeping on rollers—just three of the ways you can do your hair great damage. What does the damaged strand look like? A piece of badly knotted and horribly frayed rope!

Despite the fact that I've colored my hair for nineteen years—and had to subject it to all sorts of professional "indignities" while modeling—I've never had to invest in professional hair treatments. Furthermore I never go to a beauty salon to have my hair done. I hate beauty salons with a hot passion. Oh, there are some good salons, but they're few in number.

I used to pose for advertisements promoting the salon of a very famous New York hairdresser who would sketch the hairstyle he decided would be "in" for the new season. Then he'd instruct his staff that *this* was the style for every customer. No matter the texture of her hair or the shape of her face—*this* was the hairstyle. I suppose watching the master at work, and aware of his fancy prices and the scant attention he paid to a customer's individual needs, soured me on beauty salons in general; that, and the immense damage I've seen them do to hair: overbleaching, bad cuts, etc. etc. Perhaps I'm being unfair. I don't know. What I *do* know is that I can take care of my hair myself, and save money as a result.

Why not? Hair is so intensely personal. You must get to know and understand your own hair. Learn to recognize the signals it sends out in the form of "complaints" when it's feeling sick: split ends, spongy texture, drab color, dandruff. A woman's hair reflects the state of her health and mind, and vice versa. Naturally—hair, after all, is a living thing, part of your body. Your hair and you are a team. No woman can be 29 Forever if her hair is dull and drab. The 29 Forever spirit extends from toe tips to hair ends!

My hair care rule is simple: treat your hair as you treat your face—with tender, loving care. It works. I know. My hair is shiny and healthy. In fact, it has so much shine that sometimes when I do TV commercials, the hair stylist on the set has to powder down my hair.

Keep It Clean

How often should you shampoo? There's no hard 'n' fast rule. I say shampoo often enough to keep your hair clean. After all, that's what shampooing is all about, isn't it? Your particular hair type (oily hair, for example, needs more shampooing) and where you live will generally dictate how often you must shampoo. If you live in a big city awash with polluted air, you will have to shampoo often. *Bad Air leads to Bad Hair.* So you should wash it frequently, to cleanse it of all the soot and fumes and dust that collect in it.

I would never, under any circumstances, shampoo my long hair *every* day, but if for some reason you must, Dr. Sonia Lindo, clinical assistant professor of dermatology at Cornell Medical College, recommends a liquid castile soap or a very mild baby shampoo and "lather only once." I add, if you shampoo daily by all means use a conditioner. I do even when I shampoo every five days or so. First

107

it's the cream conditioner applied to my dripping wet hair, rinse, and next, a body builder to give it more bounce.

No matter what your shampoo timetable is (and it undoubtedly changes, depending on the season and where you're located at the time; damp and/or humid weather robs my hair of its shine in two days flat), cleaning your hair should be more than simply shampooing. It should be a bonafide beauty treatment for your scalp and tresses:

1) Begin by gently massaging your scalp to rev up circulation. Hair thrives on exercise. Your scalp is wonderfully manipulatable. So go to it—gently, but firmly. Place both palms flat on your scalp with your fingertips about an inch apart. Then push your hands toward each other so that a small part of your scalp will, so to speak, rise to the occasion. Keep moving your hands in the same position until you've covered your entire scalp, and it feels loosened. *Don't,* under any circumstances, use your nails; use the balls of your fingertips.

2) Now you're ready for brushing. A good brushing will further stimulate circulation of the scalp and lift loose dirt from your hair. But first things first; make sure you have the right kind of brush: a natural, deep-bristle brush with no sharp ends to break your hair. As for those legendary 100 strokes: forget it. Brush just enough to start your hair feeling bouncy and lively. And brush *slowly* for less possible breakage. Too much brushing and too vigorous brushing can actually wear out your hair. Since brushing helps distribute the natural oils over the entire hair shaft, oily hair can do with less brushing than dry or normal hair.

When your brush bristles encounter a tangle, gently work out the tangle with your fingers, working from the ends of your hair upwards, and then resume brushing.

Here is the very best brushing technique:

Bend over from the waist and brush back to front, up and out from the scalp right down to the very end of the hair.

While brushing, stimulate scalp circulation by clutching the hair and giving it a gentle, but firm, tug.

3) Choose a gentle shampoo specially formulated for your type of hair. Water should be lukewarm to cool, not hot. Massage your scalp with the lather, again taking care not to use your fingernails, which can cause scratches that may become infected. Use the balls of your fingertips and be sure to cover the entire scalp area. If you wash your hair often, it should take only one shampoo to get it clean. But if it needs a second, don't hesitate.

Rinse, rinse, and rinse again. Always finish with cool water to retract the hair. Rinse thoroughly. Don't leave a trace of shampoo in your hair.

4) Wet hair is weak hair. The shaft has absorbed all that water and simply isn't up to brushing while wet. I recommend that you don't rub with a towel but, instead, blot your hair dry with your towel, or wrap your head in a towel and let it drain. Then, while it's slightly damp, set it. Setting the hair while slightly damp will help to control the *frizzies*.

Keep It Healthy

All types of hair—not only damaged hair—benefit from a conditioner. Read the labels carefully and select the conditioner that seems to "speak" to your hair. Basically they all work the same way but, since they're created for different hair problems, they're sometimes used in different ways. (Some are rinsed off right away; some, after a specified time period; and some stay on to become setting lotions.) So read the directions carefully.

Now here are some tips to guide you in making the right choice:

Cream conditioners aid in the prevention, as well as correction, of hair damage. It's best to leave the cream on at least thirty minutes.

Quick rinse-out conditioners help damaged hair and leave it extra shiny and manageable.

Heat-activated conditioners are used with electric rollers to give your hair firm body and livelier, longer-lasting curls. I strongly recommend that you use electric rollers only for emergencies, and then be sure to cover the ends of your hair with tissues for protection.

Leave-in body-building conditioners are for fuller, thicker, springier hair.

Conditioners for long hair help prevent and control some special problems, such as frizzies, tangles, split ends, flyaways. They leave hair silky soft.

Always Remember:

Very hot dryers are taboo. So turn the dial to medium and hold the hand dryer a foot away from your head.

Never, but never, cut your hair with a razor; it damages the hair shaft.

Make sure *everything* you use on your hair is 100 percent clean: brushes, combs, curlers, clips, etc etc.

Make sure the teeth of your comb don't "bite" your scalp or have ragged edges that "catch" the hair. Choose one with rounded, widely spaced teeth.

Protein shampoos can help keep your hair *young*. After all, hair is 97 percent protein.

To clean your brush, place it, bristles down, in lukewarm water mixed with a little ammonia. Rinse in clear, cold water. Dry, bristles down, in a warm, dry place.

Best foods for hair are: avocado, carrot juice, asparagus, apricot, apple, liver, rice, yogurt, wheat germ, fish, chicken, green peas, spinach, whole-wheat breads and cereals. If your hair is oily, less oil in your diet will mean less oil in your hair. So avoid nuts, chocolate, butter, and fried foods.

Adding a few drops of lemon juice to your shampoo will make hair shinier.

A vinegar rinse adds extra highlights to dark hair. It works for blondes, too, but blondes should use only *white* vinegar.

Backcomb as little as possible. Best combing method: hold a handful of hair at a time and comb from the center to the ends, then scalp to center.

An occasional oil treatment is recommended as a preshampoo conditioner for dry hair. Apply warm olive oil or castor oil to the scalp with cotton balls or pads. Then wrap the head in a hot towel. Continue hot towel treatment for a minimum of twenty minutes and then remove towel and massage oil into the scalp. Wrap head in a fresh hot towel and keep it on for at least an hour. Shampoo a minimum of three times to remove all the oil.

Regardless of the length of hair or your particular hairstyle, each strand should be cut straight across rather than at an angle. Why? because the ends are the weakest part of your hair; they're not covered by a protective outer cuticle, so the hair shaft is completely exposed. Cut your hair at an angle, and what happens? The inner shaft is exposed, allowing more of that all-important protein and moisture to escape. So even if you, like I, wear your hair long, it should have the benefit of a trim—cut in this fashion—every six weeks to help keep it bouncy and manageable.

If you use a hair spray, avoid overspraying. Only the top layer of hair needs it; no need to apply it to the scalp.

Hair care is a year 'round affair. Summer sun is murder on your hair, but cold weather does its damage, too. Heads are often covered by those handsome fur chapeaux and consequently hair is squashed and less air gets to the scalp. Add to that the drying effects of steam heat indoors, and you can understand why hair grows faster in warm weather.

If your hair is dry, use a pure castile soap shampoo. If your hair is oily, use a soap-based shampoo that will provide you with a really lavish lather.

Summer Hair Needn't
Be Sad Hair

We know, don't we, the damage that sun and salt water can do to hair? I play tennis and golf, swim, water-ski, and ride horses during the summer months—and in winter, too, when I can zip off to some tropical paradise. But I take care that my hair doesn't become dry, frizzy, and sun damaged. In short I take precautionary measures, which are especially important if your hair, like mine, has been chemically treated, because then it's even more vulnerable to sun damage.

When I'm out in the sun for any length of time, I never fail to cover my head with a floppy hat or scarf. And after swimming, I immediately wash out the pool's chlorine or the ocean's salt with a mild, nondetergent shampoo followed by a protein-enriched, leave-in conditioner. Often I mix the juice of half a lemon with the rinse water to be absolutely certain every trace of chlorine or salt is washed away.

Wigs

I own several, but I have used them only on modeling assignments. I feel more like ME with my own hair. I have nothing against wigs, mind you, but I just don't feel I need one as a matter of course. Still, scores of women I know have not only one wig, but a wardrobe. That's fine, provided a wig or a collection of wigs doesn't tempt a woman to neglect her hair. And, of course, wearing a wig day in, day out, can dull hair and, in some cases, actually cause hair to fall out.

I say, look at a wig as an investment for emergencies. First, it will save you time. You have an appointment, your hair needs attention, you don't have time—and there's your wig, looking stunning and so inviting. That's just for starters. Your wig also won't turn grey; droop in damp weather; or get the frizzies on a humid day.

You don't own a wig? But you do want to buy one? Then consider these points when choosing yours.

Since this is Wig Number One, I wouldn't go wild and choose one in a startling style that's far away from the style in which you normally wear your hair. A good wig costs too much to be used as a fun fad.

Still, the beauty of a wig should be its ability to change personality. Some wigs are specially designed to be more versatile than others, to lend themselves to some dramatic changes when put in the hands of a good hairdresser. Look for one of these versatile wigs.

Consider the proportions of the wig you try on. It may look sensational from the neck up but how does it look when you stand up? Before you buy, take a long, objective look at your bewigged self in a full-length mirror.

Make sure it fits comfortably: not too loose, not too tight, but secure and comfortable. Move your head around; stand up and move your whole body around. Someone else may put it on your head the first time but, before you decide to buy, you should take it off and put it on by yourself.

Caring for Your Wig

- Like your hair, your wig should be shampooed when it becomes dull looking.
- Again, as with your hair, you should brush your wig before shampooing to loosen any hair spray and tangles. Use a wide-bristle wig brush.
- Shampoo with a recommended shampoo. Rinse. Shake. Hang to dry anywhere air can circulate. Ideally it should be put on a wig stand, because a stand will keep the base of the wig in shape. When it's perfectly dry, shake and brush. Like your hair, your wig shouldn't be combed or brushed while wet, unless you really want to take out some of its curl. Then go ahead—but gently, working from the bottom up.
- Always use wide-toothed combs.
- Never place the wig near heat or crumple it in a box. Store it in its own wig box, or put it on a wig stand. Failing that (rakish though it sounds), hang it on a doorknob.

The Question of Color

If I Have Only One Life to Live ... Let Me Live It as a ____

You fill it in—blonde, redhead, brownette, brunette.

I chose mine—blonde—eighteen years ago. I've never been sorry, because I have discovered, to my immense satisfaction, that blondes *do* have more fun. But don't let me influence you. You choose.

There's no reason in the world why you should suffer with a hair color you don't like . . . that isn't YOU. Get out from under it. Kick the dull hair habit. Choose a new color or, at the very least, a lively new shade of your natural color.

I chose blonde because I felt—and still feel—that the proper shade of blonde is immensely flattering, adding lightness to a woman's face. When I first went blonde I went *too* blonde, almost white blonde. I also made the mistake of wearing my eyebrows too heavy for a blonde look. But I quickly learned and corrected my mistakes.

There are so many shades of each hair color that your only problem will be selecting the one most flattering to you. I believe that as one grows older, a shade somewhat lighter than one's natural color is most "youthifying." Still . . .

Rose Kennedy has chosen to remain a stunning brunette. So has glamourous Merle Oberon. Gloria Swanson's hair is a sable brown, which I believe is very much like her natural color. Joan Crawford, when last I saw her, was wearing a soft beige blonde. One of the most luscious shades of red hair I've ever seen belongs to writer Helen MacInnes, whose novels of suspense have been best sellers for the past thirty-five years. Scottish born, with magnetic sapphire-blue eyes, Ms. MacInnes has refused to sacrifice her auburn hair to the calendar. Nor have

Here I am in 1940, age six.

Several years later, at a very awkward age thirteen, I'm trying hard to hide my painful shyness behind a big smile.

The smile is real this time! Being voted a high school calendar
girl seemed the most wonderful thing in the world to me.

At twenty-four, I start modeling in Florida. My mother is distressed when she sees my new blond hair.

Though I'm only twenty-six, I take my first 29 FOREVER step by leaving Florida and going to New York to model.

My first success. I look more confident and professional, but I'm still a bit surprised by all the good things that are beginning to happen to me.

MODERN
Beauty Shop

APRIL, 1965

N TWO SECTIONS · SECTION ONE

My modeling career is thriving, as you can
see from these very different looks. I've
now passed my thirtieth birthday—but
I've stopped counting since I
now know that I'm
29 FOREVER.

Here I am at thirty-five, with my twenty-six-year-old sister Francey. At thirty-five I look and feel better than I did at twenty-five.

In these shots I'm thirty-six and thirty-seven. Although I'm still modeling, I'm spending more time on my other interests.

At thirty-eight I'm happy to be able to devote more time
to my painting. And I'm delighted to be invited
to show my work in New York galleries.

The calendar now says that I'm forty.
But the woman in this picture is clearly 29 FOREVER.

At forty-one, I'm only modeling to promote my own
beauty products and enterprises.

I've never doubted for a minute that my son, David,
helps keep me 29 FOREVER.

Forty-two years
—and I'm sure that the next forty-two
will be even better!

Lucille Ball, Greer Garson, Arlene Dahl, and any number of other ravishing redheads.

Of course, I am pro-blonde. I maintain that there's a shade of blonde for every woman who wants to be a blonde. I don't promise that it will look "natural," but it will look stunning. Why must it look natural? Have you ever seen a true Scandinavian blonde with a toasty suntan? *Scrumptious.* So much then for the old bromide that only a fair-skinned, blue-eyed female looks well as a blonde! There are 1.5 million new blondes each year. Join them this year, if you want. Don't fear. Hair coloring has never been as good and as easy as it is now.

Changing your hair color will change your lifestyle—and your makeup and fashion colors, too. For example, when a woman goes blonde, she'd do well to avoid bright red or orange lipstick (unless she's under twenty-five and has a perfectly fabulous skin). After all, once you're blonde, you're already more noticeable. So your makeup must be softer, subtler. You'd probably do well, too, to avoid bright red and orange fashion colors in your wardrobe. Why compete with your beautiful new hair color? Instead play it up by wearing softer, subtler fashion colors as well.

In deciding on your new hair color, it's a good idea to try on a wig in the particular shade that intrigues you most. Study how it looks on you under *all* lighting conditions. Then, when you've made your decision, select your method of hair coloring carefully. If you're going to do the job yourself, please follow instructions on the package very, very carefully. Most directions call for two important tests: the *patch test* for allergic reactions and the *strand test* to check on how the product and shade work on your hair.

You don't have to bleach or dye all your hair. There are, for instance, halfway measures that will give you a blonde look without going completely blonde: *frosting, tipping, streaking.*

Basically there are three kinds of hair colorings: temporary, semipermanent, and permanent.

The temporary hair coloring—rinses and high-lighting shampoos—only last until your next shampoo. They don't lighten hair—they add highlights—because they contain no bleaching agents. They make only subtle changes in color, since they coat only the outside of the hair shaft. A rinse won't cover grey, but it will blend it in by adding a little color to it. It can help eliminate yellowish casts from white or grey hair.

Semipermanent hair colorings are gentle *penetrating* colors. They last through five or six shampoos. Again, they will not lighten hair color, because they contain no bleaching agents. But they will add a brightening effect, since they not only coat the hair shaft, but also gently penetrate its surface. Semipermanents come in either lotions or aerosols. Lotions are more concentrated, work faster, and make a bigger color difference. Aerosols are more diluted and have gentler effects. Both kinds, however, have conditioners added, and so give extra sheen along with extra color.

Permanent hair colorings do lighten hair, do cover grey, because they contain bleaching agents and penetrate the hair shaft. They actually strip the hair shaft of its natural color and make the hair shaft more porous, both of which make the hair more receptive to a new color; a color, by the way, that can't be shampooed out. It lasts until the hair grows out and is cut off, or you change the color again chemically.

There are one-step and two-step permanent hair colorings. The one-step will lighten and brighten by several shades, but its lightening action isn't strong enough to change, say, a dark brunette into a pale blonde. So if you're raven tressed and want to become a pale blonde—or if you want *any* dramatic change of permanent color—it's the two-step for you.

Needless to say, Oleda of the naturally medium-brown tresses does the two-step, and gladly.

Of course, going to another color means you must fuss a little more with your hair. You owe it to yourself and your public not to go around with dark roots showing. But I don't always "touch up" all my roots. About every ten days, I will put only Clairol's Extra Light A on the part, where dark roots begin to show first. (I leave it on for about an hour and fifteen minutes and then wash it off.) About ten days later, I'll color the entire new growth with bleaching and color. Next time it's only the part again. My hair grows very fast and, if I have a particularly important meeting or date, I have to color about once a week. Extra care, to be sure, but it's well worth it to be a blonde!

If you should decide to have your hair lightened to a pale blonde, it's going to pass through *five* stages of color change, one of which is a rather raucous shade of orange-gold. (It's at this temporary stage that some women panic. Don't. It's only temporary—a way station enroute to a gorgeous pale yellow.) It's important, too, that you not be too hasty in judging your new hair color. Allow a day or two to pass. Give your hair's natural oils a chance to get back in place; they'll affect the color, too. Meanwhile you can spend the time selecting some new shades of makeup that will complement your new hair color. Then with hair oils back in place, your new makeup applied, take another look in your mirror and enjoy, ENJOY!

If you'd like to lighten your eyebrows, too (they should be a shade or two darker than your hair), go right ahead. I suggest it be done by your hairdresser, but if you insist on doing it yourself, use a brow lightener and toner you can brush on.

Special Care for Colored Hair

1) Use a gentle shampoo created for hair-color users—and don't spare the suds.

2) Use a conditioner after every shampoo. It keeps colored hair beautifully manageable and lustrous.

3) Beware of strong sun, too stiff setting lotions and hair sprays. Wear a hat or scraf when in the sun, and seek out the extra-mild setting lotions and hair sprays.

Grey Hair Can Be Gorgeous

Some maintain that grey hair is always aging. I don't agree. That's a state of mind. So if your hair is greying, totally grey, or white, and you want to keep it that way, go right ahead. Make it as glamourous as it can be. And that's *plenty*.

One thing you want to avoid is any yellow discoloration. Best way to do that is to get one of Clairol's gray enhancers, Silk 'n Silver or Come Alive Gray. If your hair has lots of yellow discoloration, look for the platinum tones to help tone it down. If you want to deepen the shade of your hair and even it out, look into the smoky tones. These grey enhancers wash out (Silk 'n Silver in four to six shampoos; Come Alive Gray every time you shampoo), so you can easily change to a lighter or darker shade when you reapply.

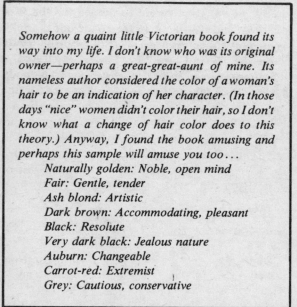

Somehow a quaint little Victorian book found its way into my life. I don't know who was its original owner—perhaps a great-great-aunt of mine. Its nameless author considered the color of a woman's hair to be an indication of her character. (In those days "nice" women didn't color their hair, so I don't know what a change of hair color does to this theory.) Anyway, I found the book amusing and perhaps this sample will amuse you too...

    Naturally golden: Noble, open mind
    Fair: Gentle, tender
    Ash blond: Artistic
    Dark brown: Accommodating, pleasant
    Black: Resolute
    Very dark black: Jealous nature
    Auburn: Changeable
    Carrot-red: Extremist
    Grey: Cautious, conservative

Your Hairstyle Can Help You Look Your Best.
Short Neck? Wear your hair at ear level or above.
Long Neck? Wear a longish style, back-brushing the entire head very gently for soft lines and fullness.
Square, Heavy-Set Face? Choose a hairstyle with height and curvy waves.
Thin, Sharp Face? A rounded hairstyle with fullness at the sides, never angled.
High Forehead? A fluffy, separated bang or a sideswept bang.
Low Forehead? Bangs for you too, but yours should be short and high rounded or separated.
Thin Hair? First things first. Get a body permanent. Next, use a body builder labeled for fine hair. Then choose a hairstyle that has more than a little curl to it.
Coarse Hair? Start with a conditioner that will help soften your hair. Then choose a hairstyle with a smooth look, setting hair only with the largest of curlers to avoid small, "busy" curls.

Long Hair After Thirty... Forty?

I'm 34, look younger than I am, and my husband prefers my hair long. I feel silly at my age with my hair this length, but what do I do? J.C.
Answer: In our opinion your hair needs cutting. It will be healthier and easy to manage if it's shorter.

I am 30 but most people think I'm in my twenties, and most of my friends actually are. Every now and then I wonder if I shouldn't "dress my age"—whatever that means. What do you think? N.S.
Answer: Fortunately, fashion hasn't been a matter

of age for a long time! Women of any age can wear most anything they like except on certain very formal or structured occasions. There's no reason why you shouldn't continue to wear what you like and feel comfortable in, now and for as long as you want. You may want to pass up the most kicky faddy clothes in preference for more classic, long-lasting styles, but that's really more a matter of the money you have to spend on clothes than of age.

Two different letters, but the same editor replying to both. I applaud her answer to N.S., but *deplore* her answer to poor J.C. Now why in the world is fashion no longer a matter of age, but hairstyling is? I'm forty-two. I wear my hair long, and I have absolutely no intention of cutting it in the foreseeable future.

When I started modeling at age twenty-six in New York City, my hair was long . . . hairstyles were short . . . and the model agency asked me to cut mine. I cut it to above the shoulder, and then I kept cutting it shorter and shorter until it ended at my earlobe. Then at twenty-nine I thought to myself: "I'd better grow my hair long again. I'll be thirty soon and I won't be able to wear it long much longer." Well in no time at all my hair was almost to my waist. That's about where it is now, at age forty-two, and that's where it's going to stay. I like it. I think long hair gives the illusion of youth, provided you've taken care of yourself, kept your skin fresh, your weight down, and your vitality UP. So there's no reason I can see for anyone to put an age limit on long hair.

Brigitte Bardot at forty-one has beautifully long, soft hair. Jackie Onassis at forty-five wears hers shoulder length and it's very much a part of her appeal. Barbara Walters, the First Lady of Television, is forty-three and wears hers shoulder length, too (and a few shades lighter), and she looks infinitely younger and more attractive than she did when she started on the Today Show with a bouffant hairstyle.

Furthermore, I don't agree with the editor's claim that shorter hair is healthier and easier to manage. Healthy hair can be any length. I find my long hair very easy to manage. If I need to set my hair in between shampoos, I simply pull it back and tie it with a ribbon. Then I take the ends of hair and roll them into a big curl and pin it up on top of my head. This curls the ends just enough, and I manufacture a perfectly nice hairstyle while I sleep.

I don't say that I'll always wear my hair as long as it is now. Someday I may cut it shoulder length. But I can promise you I'll always wear it soft (and blonde). A soft, casual hairstyle—especially if the ends turn up—makes any woman look and feel 29 Forever!

11

A Luscious, Young
Mouth—
With a voice to match

I REFUSE TO believe that a baby's earliest smiles are the result of gas. I won't even bother to check out the authenticity of that claim. I'll just go on cherishing the memory of seeing my infant son's cherubic lips part and curl into a lopsided smile. He looked so divinely happy! so at peace with the world!

At any age, a smile is the loveliest thing you can do for your face. It's the "lift" *extraordinaire*. When your smile also reveals the flash of strong, white teeth, the effect is dazzling.

Just as we must have a small but mighty arsenal of beauty aids for beautiful young hands and feet, we also need aids to insure a luscious, young, Forever 29 mouth: lipstick, lip brush, lip gloss, a soft-bristle nylon toothbrush, fluoride toothpaste, unwaxed dental floss, a mouthwash and breath freshener, a Water Pik—and your own index finger.

Lipstick and lip gloss need no explanation, don't you agree? A coat of gloss over your lipstick will

give your lips a tantalizingly moist look. A young
mouth is always fresh looking and moist. Young lips
are never dry or cracked. Nor are they thin and
pinched looking. Yet one's lips often show a marked
tendency to lose their softness and voluptuous
shape as birthdays multiply. That's when a lip brush
(or lip liner) comes into play to shape your lips as
you want them to be.

By now the value of a fluoride toothpaste should
be beyond question; also that of the fluoride
mouthwash. The more ways you use fluoride, the
less susceptible to tooth decay you and your family
will be.

As for your dental floss, use it after every meal,
whether you brush after every meal or not (if you
don't brush, then it's all the more important that
you use dental floss). Take care, however, that you
use it properly—never so vigorously that you do
damage to the tender gum tissue between your teeth.
Wrap the floss against the side of the tooth and
move it back and forth; then pull it out, taking with
it any food particles that have nestled between the
teeth. The regular use of dental floss and a Water
Pik will help keep your teeth free of plaque, the
sticky, nearly transparent film that leads to tooth
decay and gum disease.

Last, but certainly not least, is that clever index
finger of yours. Use it for gum massage. Granted
some toothbrushes have squishy rubber tips created
expressly for gum massage, but I prefer the feel of
my own fingertip. I massage across and then in the
direction of my teeth, thus working to prevent gum
erosion—your smile's worst enemy.

But none of this will work magic, unless you eat a

balanced diet. Both calcium and phosphorus are essential to strong teeth and bones. Your diet must contain adequate supplies of milk, fish, meat, cheese (opt for the lower-fat kinds: cottage, pot, and farmer), peas, and beans. I adore apples, not only for their delicious taste, but also the happy knowledge that their juice helps keep my teeth clean and free of cavities. Meantime cut down on your intake of candy, cake, cookies, and soft drinks. If you must drink soft drinks, take them through a straw that will get their sugar content past your teeth.

STOP SMOKING. It stains your teeth. And no amount of skillful brushing can really undo the damage. (Salt is very likely the most effective way to clean teeth of tea and cigarette stains.) But please don't stop smoking and then compensate for the "sacrifice" by eating candy or chewing a sugary gum. That sort of compensatory tactic all too often results in cavities.

A beautiful, winning smile doesn't necessarily demand that your teeth be perfect. Certain defects can be "interesting," even charming. Model-actress Lauren Hutton, whose annual income is well up in the six figures, has a space between her two front teeth that gives her a fetching gamine quality. (When she does her ads for Revlon, she uses caps. But when she posed for a *Newsweek* cover story and co-starred in the film *The Gambler,* she flashed her own charming, less than perfect smile.) Still, there are some defects that are disfiguring, and these should be corrected. I know. At twenty-seven, I finally did something about mine.

My teeth were strong—and crooked. One eye

tooth had perversely grown not where it should have, but in the roof of my mouth. As I matured, therefore, my gums began to develop an indentation where this tooth should have grown. Unfortunately a Miami dentist simply pulled this tooth and ultimately my teeth shifted over in order to fill in the space the eye tooth should have occupied. Sounds awful, but it really didn't look so awful. After all I was modeling, so it couldn't have been considered a disfigurement. But I was very self-conscious about my less than perfect smile. (Fortunately the high-fashion models in the late 1950's and early 1960's rarely, if ever, smiled.) It took some considerable shopping around before I managed to convince a dentist that yes, he should cap my two front teeth. The feeling then was, why drill down two "good" teeth, even if they weren't as straight as they might be. But I persisted, arguing that I wanted it done, and finally it was done and I've never regretted it. My timing was good, too, for soon afterward the oh-so-sophisticated, poker-faced look was "out," and the natural, animated look was "in." A beautiful smile was indispensable to a model; and there I was with mine intact, making it possible for me to sell everything from cosmetics to clothing on television.

But what good is a luscious, youthful mouth if, when you open it to speak, the voice that comes out shatters the whole illusion? This point leads me right into the importance of a lovely speaking voice.

Television commercials are pure gold for a model—all those lovely residual checks popping up in your mailbox. Of course you don't have to speak well to appear on television, but if you do and you deliver dialogue in a commercial, your residuals are that much bigger. So no wonder many of the top models place themselves in the hands of a vocal coach early in their careers.

Dorothy Sarnoff, a former actress and singer who runs her own Speech Dynamics and Executive Speech Services from her studio in New York City, has remarked that people will always forget what you were wearing, but will remember what you sounded like. The svelte, blonde Ms. Sarnoff maintains that nasality, stridency, and shrillness are to the ear what halitosis is to the nose. Her teaching does for your voice what the artful use of cosmetics does for your face.

Most women don't think of their voices as high pitched. To get an idea of what you sound like to others, she suggests you put your nose in the middle of an open magazine and talk into it. As your voice bounces back at you, you will have some idea how you sound to other people.

Ms. Sarnoff's book, *Speech Can Change Your Life* (Doubleday & Co., Inc., 1970), is full of tips which are designed to help you sound like the best possible you. Among her most important admonitions are the following:

Use as low a pitch as you can. To find yours, put your hand on your chest and proceed to lower your voice a half-tone at a time on the phrase, "I don't think it's going to snow," until you get uncomfortable, then go back up one tone.

Energize your voice by sitting chest up, with your solar plexis contracted toward the spine. Keep that position when you speak.

"Slow talking makes you," she says, "about as

131

fascinating as a dripping faucet. Talking too fast, on the other hand, turns people off, too." To pace yourself properly, Ms. Sarnoff suggests you test yourself by reading 170 words a minute; this is the pace you should maintain in your speech.

My Personal Hall of Fame

For the prettiest lips I nominate Zsa Zsa and Eva Gabor. Both ladies are past fifty, but their mouths are 29 Forever, so beautifully shaped and moist looking. I'm told that when Zsa Zsa appears on a television talk show, she arrives three hours early to apply her makeup, giving prime time to putting on lipstick and then polishing with gloss. I hear that Eva is into facial isometrics and, from the youthful look of her mouth, I feel certain she must do all those exercises for the lips that I've outlined in our About Face chapter.

A woman's voice should be no indication of her chronological age. Her voice should be airy and full of joy, no matter whether her calendar age is twenty, forty, or seventy. I think the prettiest, most alluring voices I know belong to Gloria Swanson, Joan Crawford, and Claudette Colbert—and their combined ages total *209 years!* But their voices are 29 *Forever.*

12

Beauty Sleep

IT'S NOT FOR nothing that for generations we've been referring to *beauty sleep*. It's no idle exaggeration, no beauty editor's deathless bon mot. Sleep and Beauty are interrelated. And the fairy tale *Sleeping Beauty* is really no fairy tale at all.

Sleep won't make you beautiful, but it certainly will help. Without cnough sleep—the right kind of sleep—a ravishing beauty will look ravaged, for how well and how long you sleep plays a powerful role in how well you look and feel.

"You look tired," says a friend in a moment of truth, gazing at you across the luncheon table. "Tired" in that case is a euphemism for haggard, old-looking. Could anything be more ego bruising? Yes—if a man were to say it. (Men usually don't. But they think it.)

A good night's sleep—the right kind of sleep— acts like a beauty tonic. You awake refreshed, rejuvenated. So often when a woman has face lift and no one's the wiser, friends regard her admiringly and ask if she's been away on vacation. "You look so...*rested!*"

But what's the right kind of sleep?

Answer: a good night's sleep. In short, whatever makes you feel refreshed and rejuvenated when you wake up.

So it's back to our philosophy of *Know Thyself.* In this instance, discover your sleep pattern. No two people sleep exactly alike. I thrive on eight hours a night. You may need less. Sleep needs vary from person to person, because body rhythms vary from person to person. It's a matter of metabolism and activity level. In fact, you may be one who insists she needs only five hours a night, and you may be right. But frankly I opt for at least seven, and so do the health researchers at the California State Health Department, who say, "If you want to live years longer and stay healthier, sleep at least seven but no more than eight hours per night." A good night's sleep not only puts sparkle in your eyes and polish on your skin, but it also keeps your brain in top working order. Since we spend approximately a third of our life asleep, we should do a good job of it, don't you think?

But what if you have trouble getting a good night's sleep? You toss and turn before you fall asleep, and then you wake up several times during the early morning hours. What to do? Well, sleep is a natural involuntary function of your body, a natural habit, so it should be as natural for you to sleep as it is for you to breathe. There are no magic tricks to induce sleep. But, according to Dr. Abraham Weinberg, co-founder of the Sleep

Therapy Center, you mustn't try to "force" sleep, because that will only intensify the problem. Your aim is to *relax*. How? Start thinking "relaxation." You can't *will* it. But you can induce it. Once a state of conscious relaxation has been attained, Dr. Weinberg suggests what is really a form of self-hypnosis or auto-suggestion:

1) Look upward, towards the ceiling, hard enough to put a slight strain on your eyeballs.

2) Next, focus your eyes inward as well as upward, as if you were trying to look at the tip of your nose. Keep breathing naturally.

3) Allow your eyelids to close slowly.

4) Count backwards from ten to one, in rhythm with your breathing.

5) At the count of one, take a very deep breath and let it out slowly.

6) Let your whole body go limp and loose. You're relaxed enough if you feel that you can barely lift an arm or leg. Enjoy this feeling for a few moments.

7) With your eyes still closed, imagine yourself asleep under the most pleasant and relaxed circumstances possible. Some people think of lying in a green field beside a running brook. Others think of themselves as floating clouds.

8) Open your eyes and stay relaxed. The chances are you will go from drowsiness to a deep sleep without even noticing. No one can determine for himself exactly when sleep begins, although the moment will register on a machine that measures brainwaves.

But, as Dr. Weinberg points out, you must first achieve a state of conscious relaxation. There are several ways of nudging yourself toward that goal. Should you need more incentive, Gayelord Hauser, the world-famous nutritionist, though he admits it takes time to learn to relax completely, goes on to say, "Relaxation is youthfulness, and when you have learned to relax your entire body at will, you will have learned the secret of youthfulness."

Some women do it by lying with their feet propped up on a pillow and cool, soothing compresses over their eyes.

Calcium is a big help. It's a sleep inducer. You might try taking calcium tablets at bedtime. Quoting Gayelord Hauser again, "Calcium means rest. Calcium means deep sleep."

Certainly the right kind of mattress is essential to the right kind of sleep. All of which means a mattress long enough and wide enough to give you stretch-out comfort, and firm enough, yet flexible enough, to "give" where it should and support where it should. Any other kind of mattress is rightly called an *aging mattress*.

Discover the nightwear that's the right wear for you. Some nightwear fabrics are very glamourous but also terribly uncomfortable, hiking up and twisting into weird folds and knots as you move about in your sleep. (During the night, we usually change position about forty times.) Your most comfortable (and glamourous) nightwear may very well be your birthday suit. If it is, then by all means sleep nude. What you wear—or don't wear—to bed counts.

Some of those women with their feet propped up and compresses over their eyes go a step further and follow the advice of Dr. David Harold Fink in his book, *Release from Nervous Tension* (Fireside, 1962) and say to themselves slowly, calmly, "Relax...let go...relax...more...more..."

Still others choose to woo relaxation via a hot tub. Like fashion designer Pauline Trigère, they regard their bath as both joy and relaxation. I know I do. I swear, if I missed mine for even one night, I couldn't sleep half as well.

Hearing is the last sense to fall asleep. So it's not surprising that there has been considerable research of late into how to use sound to help lull you to sleep. As a result Syntonic Research, Inc., has produced a series of records called *Environments,* which offers you your choice of such relaxing sounds as those of the seashore, rain in a pine forest, or crickets at dusk. Each record sells for about $6, and you can get them at major record stores or by writing: Syntonic Research, Inc., 175 Fifth Avenue, New York, New York 10010.

When everything—mattress, nightwear, etc.—are the way they should be, top it all off with a sleep-inducing drink; perhaps a glass of warm milk with a dash of honey. A favorite of mine is a glass of warm milk sweetened with a teaspoon of blackstrap molasses. (Molasses is rich in magnesium, which is a natural tranquilizer.) Delicious...soothing...and what a wonderful way to down those calcium tablets!

Still another soothing hot drink is a combination of fresh orange and herb milk. Somewhat more complicated than my warm milk/molasses combo, but why not alternate them?

Hot Orange-Herb Milk

1 cup milk
1 slice orange
1 tbsp. nonfat dry milk solids (optional)
1 tbsp. honey
1 cinnamon stick
1 filter bag camomile flowers

Simmer first five ingredients for three minutes. Bring to a boil and strain into a mug containing camomile bag. Cover and let stand two minutes. Remove filter bag. Garnish hot drink with orange slice and cinnamon. Sip slowly.

Last but not least (certainly not least!), if you sleep with someone you love, chances are you'll sleep well. New research findings indicate that Sex and Sleep, like Beauty and Sleep, interact. In their book *Human Sexual Inadequacy* Dr. William H. Masters and Virginia E. Johnson suggest that chronically impotent men and nonorgasmic women often have sleeping problems. In short, poor sex and poor sleep often go hand in hand.

In a sleep experiment conducted at the University of Illinois College of Medicine in Chicago, couples who were accustomed to sleeping together in the same bed were separated for one or two nights. It was found that they became anxious and displayed disturbed sleep patterns.

So while much of this research attempting to establish a clinical connection between Sex and Sleep is still theoretical—sex research and sleep research both being relatively new areas of study—it is generally believed that the same personality factors that keep some persons from letting themselves go sexually also keep them from letting themselves drift off into sleep.

As for me, I do believe that two can sleep better than one. Since good Sleep and good Sex are both essential to remaining 29 Forever, and both are nocturnal habits (usually) practiced in private (I should hope so), and usually on a bed, I do think it behooves us to consider that, more often than not, you can't have one without the other!

13

Eat and Grow Younger

To be 29 Forever, you must eat a balanced diet. An unbalanced diet speeds up the so-called aging process.

"Any woman can be beautiful all her life with just a small effort," declares Eva Gardiner, a beauty consultant at the Max Factor Studio in London. Among other things, Ms. Gardiner recommends you "get plenty of sleep and exercise, and eat regular well-balanced meals, as I always do." You look at this awesomely lovely woman who is sixty and looks decades younger, and you're *convinced.*

If you have, like many people, learned foolish dietary habits, you must start to unlearn them—and replace them with sensible dietary habits. That does NOT mean stuffing one day and starving the next. What it does mean is learning something about nutrition so that you give your body the foods it needs in order to function at peak performance. Nutrition is so important to good health that, while addressing the fifty-seventh annual meeting of The American Dietetic Association in Philadelphia, Senator Richard Schweiker of Pennsylvania, who is on both the health committee and the select committee on nutrition and human needs, urged that all medical schools set up nutrition education programs.

"I'm amazed at the ignorance of nutrition among adult Americans," says Dr. Jean Mayer, the renowned Harvard University nutritionist. Maintaining that "Good eating habits make for healthy people," Dr. Mayer says he believes that no one should be allowed to graduate from high school without having had a solid course in nutrition.

I have little respect for women who prefer to remain dumb about nutrition, for she's doing damage to herself and her family. I'm particularly impatient with the women who gorge themselves fifty weeks a year, and then jet off to a beauty spa where they're pampered like infants. For two weeks they give up smoking and drinking, eat sensibly, exercise regularly, and come home looking and feeling rejuvenated—only to resume their smoking, drinking, and overeating. The following year, off to the beauty spa again—like a guilt-ridden child who nevertheless enjoys all the attention her naughtiness wins her. One wealthy woman I once knew summed it up, I think, when she said (in an aren't-I-a-naughty-girl manner), "The dieting does take off a few pounds. And the exercise certainly does tone up my muscles. But it's the pampering that I really love."

That's not to imply that you have to be rich to be purposely dumb about nutrition. There are millions of women of limited income who squander their food budget dollars on high-calorie, low-energy foods.

By the time I graduated from high school in Miami, I already knew more than a little about nutrition. Not courtesy of a teacher or teachers, but rather courtesy of my father. Today, age sixty-eight, my father looks and feels radiantly healthy. And here am I—forty-two—and I am told I look so much younger. The publishers of my last beauty book received so many letters accusing them of publishing lavishly retouched pictures of me that they added this line to all advertisements carrying my photographs: "This is a totally *unretouched* photo of forty-two-year-old Oleda Baker."

I can't remember when I didn't snub a slice of spongy white bread for a slice of more nourishing bread; or, whenever possible, spurn a spoonful of white sugar for a spoonful of pure honey or unrefined sugar; when I didn't pass up potato chips for, say, a handful of raisins or carrot sticks. So you see, I've never had foolish dietary habits to unlearn. Nor have my sisters. Just listen to them:

Carmen: "What do I eat? The main thing is what I don't eat. White table sugar is the villain in our house. It is anathema! It's like the plague or treated so. I cook, bake, and sweeten with honey."

Francey: "Why are some parents 'lucky' to have children who like to eat the right things, while other parents bemoan the fact that their children only like hot dogs? There are several factors involved: the parents' eating habits; atmosphere of the home (whether there is constant bickering or a pleasant environment); the creativity of parents in preparing dishes; the manner in which food is served (including the size of portions). All of these factors help condition a child to either accept or reject new tastes and new feelings in his mouth." (You'll notice that Francey doesn't refer to the creativity of mother in preparing dishes, but rather "the creativity of *parents.*" Ms. Francey is a naturally liberated female.)

All right, you say, exactly what is a balanced diet?

Answer: a balanced diet is one that feeds you ENERGY instead of "EMPTY" calories.

In the words of Dr. Henry W. Sebrell, a nutrition authority who for more than a dozen years was head of Columbia University's Institute of Human Nutrition, it is a diet that is "the right balance and amounts of protein, carbohydrates, fat, vitamins, and minerals. This is the only way to stay at the height of vitality."

Dr. Frederick Stare, of the Harvard School of Public Health, is even more specific. He says that a balanced diet is one that includes fruits and vegetables, cereals, some milk, and small servings of lean meat, chicken, and fish. In short, a diet that concentrates on canny nutrition, not deprivation.

Eat and Grow Younger simply means Eat Young. You'll never go hungry—far from it. Low-calorie foods aren't less tasty than high-calorie foods. Often they're much tastier.

When the late Elizabeth Arden opened her celebrated Arizona Maine Chance in Phoenix many years ago—250 acres resplendent with giant cactuses, palm trees, citrus trees, manicured lawns, and beautiful rose gardens—she commissioned

144

nutritionist Gayelord Hauser to design a diet that was low in calories, but also nutritious and delicious. He did, and those same nutritious, delicious, low-calorie foods are available in your supermarket.

Let me give you a few examples of how very easy it is to save calories, once you become calorie conscious. (I urge you to invest in a good calorie counter. One tiny enough to slip into your handbag, so when you're dining out in a restaurant or shopping for groceries, you can peek at it and choose accordingly.)

A cheeseburger with catsup weighs in at 470 calories
A bacon, lettuce, and tomato sandwich adds up to 350 calories
Save 120 calories
A cup of vichyssoise totals 275 calories
A cup of consommé, 30 calories
Save 245 calories
A slice of apple pie gives you 350 calories
A small dish of ice cream, 160 calories
Save 190 calories

You really don't deprive yourself. You simply substitute an equally tasty low-calorie food for a tasty high-calorie food.

"Never skip a meal," advises Dr. Sebrell, recommending a big breakfast, hearty lunch, and a light dinner as an eating pattern that should become a way of life for you.

Why a light dinner? Because you gain weight by storing energy that you don't use up. So when you eat a big dinner only a few hours before retiring, you are asking your body to bank the food energy. Energy stored becomes body fat.

Dr. Sebrell recommends a big breakfast because you need the energy, since the last time you ate was actually the night before. Skip or skimp on breakfast and you'll feel wrung out by midmorning—and ravenous by evening. Dr. Sebrell wants you to take your big meals during the day, when you're most active, and need and use the energy.

Now let me give you a sample of what constitutes a big breakfast, hearty lunch, and light dinner— three delicious meals, high in energy, that still add up to only 2,000 calories. (If you're out to shed pounds and you're in good health, you very likely can not only survive, but *thrive,* on 1,000 calories a day. But as I've said earlier, that is strictly up to you and your physician. You should have a complete checkup before you begin any reducing diet.)

Breakfast

Fruit or juice
Cereal and milk
One egg, cooked any way you want
Toast, whole grain or enriched. With butter or
    margarine, jelly or honey if you wish.
Milk, a glass of whole, skim, or buttermilk

(If you're out to shed poundage, I'd choose to cut my toast and butter in half, and I'd make that a glass of skimmed milk, which is 80 calories vs. 160 for whole milk.)

Lunch

Soup or juice, optional

Meat, or protein main dish (soufflé, baked beans, seafood simply prepared)

Vegetable, a green one. Or a yellow one.

Salad, or sliced tomato as a change

Bread and butter or margarine. One slice.

Fruit, or even a light dessert—gelatin, pound cake

½ glass milk (may be skipped if milk is part of other foods)

Dinner

Juice, or clear soup

Chicken, veal, or fish. A lean portion, three or four ounces.

Vegetable, yellow or green. Or a salad.

Bread, one enriched or whole-grain slice—one pat butter only

Butter or margarine, optional

Fruit for dessert

Tea or coffee

A big breakfast is just what the doctor ordered. But if you're in a terrific hurry one morning, there's no reason why you have to skimp on this all-important meal. When I'm in a hurry, I toss my breakfast into a blender and out it comes—high in energy and so easy to drink down. A timesaver that gives me the protein and vitamins I need:

½ cup yogurt
½ banana, sliced
4 tbsp. wheat germ
1 tbsp. honey
1 whole egg
1 cup orange juice

To whip up some variety in your blender, you might like to substitute skimmed milk for the juice, and berries in lieu of the banana. Never, but *never,* forget the honey; I'm told that young tennis whiz Chris Evert gets her natural sugar energy from honey—takes it right out onto the tennis court along with her racquet.

If you use just a little bit of ingenuity, you'll find lots of ways to cut down on calories without feeling even a teeny bit deprived. There are several easy steps you can take in preparing food to cut out unneeded calories:

—Before you cook meat, make sure that you've trimmed *all* the fat from it.

—If you're frying meat, use one of the pans with a nonstick finish to cut down on the need for fat. If you don't have a nonstick pan, sprinkle the bottom of the regular pan with salt.

—Broiling meat will render more fat than frying. Broil meat whenever possible—even as a first step before adding to stews.

—When you've made a stew, sauce, or soup, refrigerate it. Then you can remove the congealed fat before reheating and serving.

—Never sauté vegetables in butter or oil. Steam them in a small amount of water (add herbs if you wish) or bouillon.

—Making a fruit glaze for meat? Choose the fruits that are packed in water or natural juice instead of those that come in heavy syrup.

—Low-calorie salad dressings should be used not only in salads, but in the preparation of marinades for meat and poultry. Not only do marinades make food tastier, they eliminate the need to use fat in cooking.

—When you broil or bake fish, substitute wine, lemon juice, or bouillon for butter.

—If you're serving tuna, always choose the kind that's packed in water instead of oil.

—Substitute low-calorie commercial mayonnaise for the regular kind.

—Yogurt or cottage cheese can replace sour cream or mayonnaise in dips and dressings. Always serve vegetables with dips in addition to high-calorie crackers and chips.

—Don't use bread in stuffings for meat, poultry, or fish. Make a vegetable stuffing—or substitute vegetables for a portion of the bread.

—Whenever you get the chance, use skim milk (liquid or dry) instead of milk or cream.

—Make your own desserts and salads with unflavored gelatin, instead of the higher calorie packaged and sweetened gelatin.

—Get in the habit of always "thinking calories." Wouldn't broiled pork chops be just as tasty as breaded ones? Won't an open-face sandwich be just as satisfying as a closed one?

Do You Still Need Vitamins?

If you know something about nutrition and calories, do you still need store-bought vitamins? Dr. Sebrell says, "You'll get all the nutritional essentials if you eat all the varieties of food good nutritionists recommend." But he adds, "The trouble is, most of us can't eat every meal in circumstances we can control. For example, it's best to have one liver meal a week. When you skip that liver meal, you skip a lot of vitamins. It's insurance, then, to take a maintenance vitamin pill each day."

According to Dr. Carlton Fredericks, a nutritionist, writer, and broadcaster for many years, "Vitamins are like a fire insurance." He opts for any number of vitamins, among them Vitamin E, which he says helps retard aging.

Basha Pudin, a stunning television model, agrees. She says she not only takes Vitamin E orally each day, but also pierces Vitamin E capsules and applies the oil to her face, especially around the eyes. Now, of course, you can get any number of creams and lotions containing Vitamin E. Basha says the secret with vitamins is knowing when and how to use them.

"Taking vitamins, as with anything else, is

relative and conditional," is the opinion of Gloria Swanson. "There's no set pattern for anyone." Whichever vitamins she takes, they have to be natural vitamins, which means organically grown. (But some physicians and nutritionists contend that there's no difference between organic and synthetic vitamins, except price—the organic ones cost more.)

The fabulously successful poet-lecturer Rod McKuen opts for Vitamin E. He admits he isn't sure it does anything, but he takes "a handful now and then just in case."

Joanne (Mrs. Paul Newman) Woodward says, "My children go off to school every morning not only with a hot breakfast, but with sixteen vitamin pills apiece and a spoonful of wheat germ oil."

Veteran actor Bob Cummings and his wife spend a reported $1,400 a year on vitamins. The sixty-three-year-old actor, who looks years younger, takes 154 natural vitamins a day, and his wife swallows 100. Even their five-year-old son pops in forty vitamin pills a day. Mrs. Cummings, an enchanting girl from Taiwan, says she regards vitamins as a health and beauty "bargain."

Actor-comedian Red Buttons is convinced vitamins pulled him through a serious illness a few years ago, and today he totes a popcorn bag full of vitamins wherever he goes. A writer for *The New York Times* noted that the very virile movie actor Charles Bronson is quite docile about following his wife's instructions "about taking the proper vitamins with just the tiniest little bit of food."

No question about it, we Americans are vitamin-happy. Pharmacists report new sales records.

Young people are going for Vitamin A because they hear it's good for acne. Vitamin C, of course, is just about everyone's favorite way of preventing colds, and sales have all but tripled in the past two years. Vitamin E is the newest glamour vitamin since we hear it's great for circulation, skin, and sex. Not to mention that in some quarters it's being touted as a means of offsetting the ill effects of air pollution. Table follows:

Is it possible to take too many vitamins? It is. The Food and Drug Administration has decided that a huge dosage of some vitamins is dangerous, and has established a Recommended Daily Allowance for store-bought, nonprescription vitamins. Vitamins containing more than 150 percent of the recommended daily allowance (RDA) must be classified as a drug. Also, some vitamins are cumulative and can be dangerous if overused.

In other words, vitamin-taking has become controversial. While I prefer to get mine from food rather than pills, I now take Vitamin C as a cold preventive and E appears to have a soothing effect on a red-eye problem I've had at times.

Whether or not you need vitamin pills as a dietary supplement is for you and your physician to decide. Meanwhile here is a Vitamin and Mineral Chart to guide you in getting the vitamins and minerals you need from the food you eat.

Vitamins and Minerals

Vitamin	Sources	The Right Amount	Too Much
A	Green, leafy vegetables, milk, egg yolk, liver, yellow vegetables and fruits, sweet potatoes, squash, peaches, apricots, most cheeses.	Promotes healthy bones, teeth, skin and eyes.	Hair may begin to thin. Loss of appetite. Swelling over bones of arms and legs.
B family	Liver, kidney, loin of pork, roast leg of mutton, yogurt, whole-wheat cereals and breads, rice, wheat germ, brewer's yeast, fish, molasses, soybeans, almonds, egg yolk, dried skim milk.	Maintains normal vision. Keeps skin healthy. Soothes nerves.	No problem.
C	Citrus fruits, berries, melons, spinach, cauliflower, red and green peppers, asparagus, endive, avocado, peaches, soybeans, green lima beans, cabbage, turnips.	Promotes healthy teeth, gums, bones, skin, nails, and blood vessels. Helps heal wounds. Most recently, it is claimed to prevent colds.	Has been known to have caused diarrhea, and some researchers suspect that high dosages may be a contributing factor to kidney stones.

Vitamin	Sources	The Right Amount	Too Much
D	Sunshine, milk, butter, egg yolk, caviar.	Promotes strong teeth and bones.	Can cause drowsiness, nausea, loss of appetite, upset stomach, headache, and demineralization of bones.
E	Liver, fish, chicken mayonnaise, margarine, wheat germ, oatmeal, brown rice, lentils, peanuts, unsalted nuts.	It's agreed this is an essential vitamin, but exactly what it does for us humans (it has an antisterility action in animals) is still not understood. Some beauty experts claim it staves off wrinkles. Elsewhere it's touted as important for a strong heart, good muscle tone, and a healthy sex life.	So far there's nothing known on this score.

K	All green leafy vegetables.	Promotes normal blood-clotting.	No problem.
P	Citrus fruits, green peppers.	Valuable to normal blood pressure.	No problem.

Mineral	Sources	The Right Amount	Too Much
Calcium	Milk (whole or skim), cheese, blackstrap molasses, figs, cabbage, beans, lentils, cauliflower, bone meal.	Builds bones and teeth. Important in function of heart muscles and nerves.	A chance of excessive calcification.
Iodine	Seafood, sea salt, and iodized salt.	Helps prevent goiter.	Too much salt can increase blood pressure.
Iron	Liver, kidneys, red meat, parsley, oysters, apricots, prunes, raisins, peas, blackstrap molasses, wheat germ, spinach, oatmeal.	Essential in forming red blood cells.	A change in skin pigmentation. Liver damage.
Magnesium	Soybeans, cocoa, egg yolk, nuts, whole-grain foods.	Acts as a natural tranquilizer, and helps build strong teeth and bones.	May lead to weakness and sleepiness.

Mineral	Sources	The Right Amount	Too Much
Phosphorus	Egg yolk, breads, cereals, nuts, meat, dairy products, beans, lentils.	Performs the same functions as calcium, and is an energy builder as well.	No problem.
Sodium and Chloride	Table salt is a mixture of sodium and chloride. Sodium is also found in clams, oysters, wheat germ.	Regulates the body's water retention. Chloride also plays a part in production of digestive juices.	Too much salt can increase blood pressure.
Potassium	Chicken, beef, pork, veal, bananas, pineapple, orange juice, broccoli, Brussels sprouts.	Regulates water retention. Influences muscular activity.	May cause mental confusion, slowing of the heart, and numbness of arms and legs.

14

... With an Assist from Mother Nature

WE ALL KNOW how vital fresh fruits and vegetables are to a balanced diet. But do you know what a fresh lemon straight from the tree (or fruitstand) can do as a natural beauty product? or an avocado? cucumber? even the potato?

Well, the cosmetic tycoons know. You bet they do. That's why they've been adding all sorts of delicious, nutritious fruits and vegetables to their beauty products. All of which behooves us to take a tour of our kitchens, and get a clearer picture of what superb beauty aids we have there, just waiting to be used. For instance...

Apples Their juice actually makes a superb skin lotion that will not only cleanse the pores, but firm the facial contours. There's more than one way to juice an apple. You can, of course, slice it and put the slices directly onto the face, but the amount of juice is limited. The other, juicier, method is to slice the apple, put slices into a blender, and then strain.

Avocados This is a lubricating fruit, rich in Vitamin E. So blend an avocado into pulp and apply it to your throat. Then cover with absorbent cotton saturated with skimmed milk, and leave on for about one hour. Do this every day for a week and the skin of your throat will look smoother, firmer. Avocado paste is also touted as a body builder for hair. Make the paste by mixing the pulp in a little water. Then use it when you shampoo. Here's how: wash your hair once to get it clean. Then apply the paste to the hair. Leave it on for five minutes and then shampoo lightly again. Rinse thoroughly.

Bananas Is your complexion dry and taut after a summer of too much sun? If it is, make two tablespoons of pulp by mashing ripe bananas. Beat in a half-teaspoon of cream and rub it on your just-cleansed skin. Leave on for half an hour and rinse off with alternate applications of warm and cool water.

Carrots Purée a carrot in your blender and add some safflower oil to the resulting pulp. Apply around the eyes to fight eye-area wrinkles.

Cucumbers Peel it, boil peelings in small amount of water, and then rub on your face. Their juice will do lovely things for oily skin and enlarged pores.

Grapes A natural moisturizer. The juice of white grapes is said to be especially soothing to dry or wrinkled skin.

Honey Here is a good facial recipe: Mix one part honey with nine parts witch hazel, put it in a tightly lidded jar, and keep in the refrigerator. Shake well before using. Apply, leave on for fifteen minutes, then RINSE WELL. The combination makes an especially refreshing pickup for your complexion.

Lemons Slice a fresh lemon into your warm-water bath, or, if you prefer, strain a full cup of fresh lemon juice and pour it in. Fresh lemon juice will reduce skin oiliness, and keep soap film from clinging to your skin.

To bleach or soften red, rough elbows: slice a lemon in half and sit with each elbow resting on a half for about ten minutes.

To bleach freckles: apply slightly salted lemon juice like a lotion, three times daily.

To remove stains and make your teeth look whiter: cut off a strip of the peel and rub it across your teeth.

Of course, lemon makes a wonderful hair rinse for blondes, both the natural and the self-made variety. Strain the juice of two lemons through cheesecloth. Mix with an equal amount of luke-warm water. Don't rinse out the solution unless your hair happens to be dry; then rinse out with clear, cool water.

Oatmeal A wonderful dry shampoo. Just massage a handful into your hair: yellow oatmeal for dark hair, white oatmeal for blonde. Then brush your hair until it shines and all the oatmeal is gone.

Oranges Their Vitamin C content helps prevent aging of the skin on neck and shoulders, leaving it looking and feeling refreshed.

Potatoes Grated potato placed around the outside of the eyes and over the lids smooths tired and delicate tissues. Cut a potato in half and rub over your hands to soften them. Raw potato applied to your elbows removes dry skin; applied to your face, it removes dead skin cells and dirt, while also helping clear skin blemishes.

Strawberries   If you have oily skin, smear a few crushed strawberries on your face and let them dry. Rinse off with lukewarm water. Nibble a few just before retiring and their high iron content will help lull you to sleep.

15

How "Scentuous" Can You Get?

PLENTY, I HOPE.

For far too long we American women have been positively prim about using scent; content with a delicate dab of perfume behind the ears (actually not a good place, since the body oil there is different from other parts of the body and so negates the scent), and perhaps a touch at the cleavage when we've felt more daring. Compared to, say, the fashionable Parisienne who leaves a trail of heavenly scent everywhere she goes, we've got a lot of catching up to do.

Scent is essential to remaining 29 Forever.

I have six bottles of perfume on my dresser at this moment. It's nine in the morning and I not only smell divine, but so does the room in which I sit. I smell something like a dahlia. The room smells like a fresh peach, which is as it should be since the walls are painted an early morning shade of yellow, a scrumptiously plush salmon carpet covers the floor, and, if you were to slice open a fresh peach, you'd see sister hues of both.

"To walk into a room that smells the way it looks is wonderful," says Amelia Bassin, the clever young witch who taught me to use scent as an accessory to home decor. In this instance, I use it to underscore a color scheme that helps to bring a touch of the outdoors, indoors.

Bloomingdale's department store is only a few blocks from my East Side apartment, and like just about everybody else in New York, I make regular pilgrimages there to buy, to look, to be looked at. "Bloomie's" is not just a giant, exciting department store. It's a way of life, a state of mind. And when new furniture display rooms are unveiled on the fifth floor, it's akin to the opening of a new production on Broadway. You can imagine the excitement when, late this past summer, new rooms were unveiled that not only looked devastatingly smart, but also "wore" scents that complemented the decor.

Each room was decorated to express the personality of a specific U.S. city, and "wore" a regional fragrance as well. New York, my home base, smelled like a mixture of chrome and plexiglass. Atlanta was a fragrant mix of camellias and gardenias. Sante Fe carried a waft of cactus and prairie brush. Hawaii suggested a nose-tingling combination of exotic flowers and moist green leaves. San Francisco put you at the foot of a pier with the tang of the sea and a velvet fog caressing your nostrils. Muntonville, New Hampshire brought me back to childhood with its smell of apples cooking.

Up until then, I'd been using fresh flowers to scent my apartment. (I was particularly partial to lilies—a heavenly scent!) When I was out of fresh flowers, I'd line shelves with scented paper. From time to time, my sheets have been sprayed with a favorite cologne. I also scent the drawers where I keep lingerie, scarves, and handkerchiefs. I've even wiped my telephone with a soft cloth dampened with cologne; and I've been known to do the same for the light bulbs in my bedside lamp. I don't deny it; I'm a fragrance "freak." So when I saw and smelled those six display rooms, I was hooked. I immediately bought a tall, slim spray can of one of the room scents created by Ms. Bassin, and now I have a living room that smells like a luscious fresh peach!

But of course, it's *your* perfume, *your* cologne, *your* fragrant talc that is most important. The 29 Forever woman wouldn't dream of starting—or ending—her day without expressing herself via a scent.

Since no woman feels the same every day (or even every hour of the same day), why confine yourself to one scent, year after year, month after month, day after day? Perhaps you feel sporty one day, sophisticated the next; shy in the morning, but seductive by dusk. There's a perfume that can underscore each mood.

Let me give you an example of how sensitively *scentuous* some women are. A model friend of mine changed her hairstyle from an elegant, simple pageboy to a flirtatious, curly one. She took one look at her mirrored image, decided she felt "curly" all over, and went right out and bought an entirely different dress from the one she had planned to wear that evening and invested in a new perfume, too. One that fit her new "curly" personality.

How do you know which perfume expresses you? I think to find out you must start at the beginning: understand the qualities implicit in each of the basic types of scent.

The florals: Ultrafeminine and nostalgic. There are some florals that express a single scent, like that of the rose or dahlia; others that are a kind of bouquet of several floral scents. When I'm feeling quiet, thoughtful—perhaps more than a little vulnerable—I choose a floral scent.

The woodsy scents: Clear, uncomplicated, refreshing; I opt for a woodsy-mossy scent when I'm preparing for a business luncheon, or when I'm in a sporty mood.

The fruits: Crisply citrus or sweet and mellow—take your pick. I call these my summer scents. Don't ask me why (I don't know), but I wouldn't wear a fruit perfume if I were trying to attract a man, but I most certainly would wear one after I had fallen in love with him. When I'm going barefoot or wearing sandals in the summer, I like to spray a fruit scent on the soles of my feet.

The exotics: Heady, intoxicating, high voltage—when you're feeling seductive and don't fear the consequences, this is your perfume. You should apply it from the toes up to all the pulse points: wrists, throat, bosom, inner arms, above your heart, a generous dab between the breasts, back of your neck, the backs of your knees, and on the soft skin between your thighs.

Now with a range of scents like that, it most

certainly takes more than flowers to create a perfume. Raw materials fall into two groups: natural and synthetic. The naturals come from all over the globe: roses from Bulgaria . . . vanilla from Madagascar . . . jasmine from Italy . . . and patchouli from India and Singapore; and that's just for starters. Animals contribute, too: the musk deer of Tibet, the civet cat found in Ethiopia, as well as the sperm whale. They all contribute vital materials. There are about 3,000 synthetic ingredients that make a contribution, too. No wonder perfume is the strongest and most lasting of scents, with toilet water usually in the second place, and cologne after that. (I say *usually,* because some colognes may be diluted versions of perfume, and when they are, they're usually more potent than a toilet water.)

Now, with that mini-encyclopedic knowledge stored in your head, here is the authoritative way to go about choosing your perfume.

Never try more than three scents at any one time. And *take your time* choosing yours. Apply one drop of each scent on a pulse point (the wrists are most often used, for the obvious reason that it can be done without disrobing and is easily accessible for sniffing). Wear them for an hour; give your body time to bring out the full power of the scent. And remember: every fragrance smells different on each individual because of its interaction with your body oils. Therefore what smells devastatingly attractive on one woman may be something less than alluring on another. So *never* buy a perfume simply because you've admired it on someone else.

Once you've chosen your scent(s), you must take proper care of them. Keep them in a dark, cool place. Avoid permitting sunshine or strong artificial light to bathe the bottle, for light can cause a chemical reaction and sometimes even change the fragrance. Avoid, too, exposing perfume to extremes of heat or cold, either of which can affect the oh so delicate balance of the scents.

Your perfume is precious, so use it wisely.

If you have oily skin, your scent will cling to you longer and so you needn't use quite as much as those women who have dry skin.

I find an atomizer is the best way to apply perfume. The spray diffuses the alcohol, enveloping your skin with a lovely light mist that lasts longer than a dab applied with the fingertips.

When a perfume bottle is empty, it isn't *kaput*. Don't toss it out. Slip it in among your lingerie and let what whispers of fragrance remain work their magic.

I wouldn't dream of traveling without my scents, any more than I'd travel without my passport or travelers' checks. Take yours in either a small aerosol or in a *well-sealed* bottle; not a plastic bottle, since scents tend to evaporate through plastic. It would be wise to keep your perfume in a *sealed* plastic bag when traveling (particularly by plane) as perfume has an uncanny way of escaping its bottle to stain its surroundings.

How long does a fragrance last on your skin? Usually the scent remains no more than four hours, which means you must reapply it or risk losing your perfume personality.

Is perfume an aphrodisiac? In a way it is, because the effect is the same when you combine a satiny-soft skin with a heavenly fragrance, and put a man within sniffing distance. In a situation like that a woman—no matter what her age—doesn't feel a day over 29!

How to introduce a little girl to perfume

All little girls are enchantingly sensuous human beings. Surely the sense of smell should be encouraged very early. A child will adore cuddling up to you and savoring your perfume. That's one way to make her aware of fragrance. But the best way I know is to show a little girl how to make her very own perfume:

Place a thin layer of pure lard on a piece of glass. Then cover the lard very lightly with flower petals. (Be sure to let the child select the flowers.) Now store the glass, with lard and petals in place, in a dark, cool spot for twenty-four hours. Then take off the petals and replace them with a fresh batch of petals, again being very careful not to press them into the lard. Keep repeating this process for several days, after which you will heat the lard just enough to melt it. Measure it and mix in an equal amount of ethyl alcohol.

Now comes the bottling. The cap of the bottle must be tightly closed. Store it for two or three weeks and then pour off the scented alcohol. Voilà! Her very own perfume! (Homemade perfumes don't retain their fragrance for very long, so use it up quickly. But then, with an excited little girl around, is there any question that it will be used up quickly?)

16

How Your Sex Life
Affects the Way You Look,
Feel, and Think

I DON'T SAY you must have an active sex life to be happy. I've known a few happy-as-a-lark celibates. I've even known a few marriages in which sexual relations played little or no part at all, and the partners—who loved and respected each other— were divinely happy. There are exceptions, you see. I'm not saying you can't be happy without Sex . . . it's just that you'll be twice as happy *with* Sex.

Sex is natural, a normal biological process. It relaxes you. It pleasures you. It *beautifies* you. In short, Sex is good for you. I regard it as one of the most dazzlingly satisfying ways I know of to remain 29 Forever.

Sex itself—the act of intercourse—hasn't changed over the ages, but our approach to the sex act has. It's certainly different today from the attitudes of thirty, twenty, even ten years ago. Still, you may be holding on to a few of those old Sexual

Myths that you heard as a child or young adult. Now is the time to blow the dust off them, expose them to the light, and see how really foolish they are. In short, let's start debunking some of the bunk about Sex!

For instance...

Sexual appetite decreases with age. BUNK! This probably shouldn't be dignified with a rebuttal. It's that foolish. Dr. William Masters and Virginia Johnson, the medical investigators, concur that the capacity to enjoy sexual intercourse in no way decreases with the years, but rather is usually retained well into extreme old age. A human being *never* loses his or her sexual urge. That urge is an impulse towards orgasm. So why should you settle for less?

If you don't achieve orgasm, fake it. Nonsense! It's nothing to be ashamed of if you don't have an orgasm, so why should you fake it? Why play games? For men an orgasm is a biological necessity; not so for women. Still, why deny yourself? You *deserve* orgasm. It's the very highest form of sexual satisfaction and there are precious few women who can't achieve it, with or without a partner—though I'm all for the former. An orgasm is an orgasm, whether it occurs during sexual intercourse, masturbation, or any other form of stimulation.

Masturbation is shameful. Better to be frustrated than masturbate. Nonsense! Masturbation is a form of sexual gratification that is neither shameful nor harmful. Furthermore, if a woman does have a problem achieving orgasm, masturbation can be a very sensible way for her to discover what excites her most. This self-knowledge can be used to help her toward achieving orgasm as often as she likes—with or without a partner! Sex is better emotionally and psychologically with a partner, but "beauty wise," the body doesn't know the difference.

Men and women are so different biologically that their responses to sexual intercourse are extremely difficult. I've always regarded this notion as something that fearful, sexually insecure members of both sexes use to hide behind. Successful lovemaking begins with excitement and ends with excitement—a total of four states—and the research of Dr. Masters and Mrs. Johnson found that the similarities in sexual response between men and women more than outweigh the differences. What are some of those differences? Well, men are aroused more quickly. But then a woman can experience a series of orgasms in fairly rapid succession, which is something few men can do.

There is only one position for sexual relations. The male mounts the female and... *Come now!* That is as foolish a notion as the idea that there is a time (nighttime) and a place (bed) for Sex... and that's that. BUNK! Fortunately more and more we are shying away from a casually smug use of the word "normal." Lovemaking asks for intelligence and imagination. Or, if you prefer, abandon. What was once condemned as an act of perversion today may be regarded as a refinement of technique.

In Japan, for instance, there is the tradition of leaving under the pillows of a newly married couple a book illustrated with pictures of all the methods and positions which might help them find sexual happiness. All too often love relationships grow dull and listless simply because the couple does not progress sexually. They're bored with the sameness of their lovemaking, but too embarrassed to discuss their boredom and experiment with new techniques. Often a woman who has a problem achieving orgasm reaches climax with fresh, new excitement via a new lovemaking technique.

Now there's one point I should like to make: don't ever feel guilty about spending time on beauty and sex. For they go hand in hand. And not only does a happy sex life help you realize your full beauty potential, but it has also been proven that it can extend your life span. Paul Niehans, the Swiss doctor noted for his work in the field of longevity research, believed that longevity is related to the secretions of the endocrine glands, more notably the sexual glands. And, of course, longevity goes hand in hand with good health.

So, decide right here and now to get ready and let yourself go so that you can become the most beautiful, radiantly healthy "you" ever!

17

The Female Orgasm

NOT TOO MANY years ago an orgasm was something a nice woman didn't have. She was just supposed to suffer through sexual intercourse, because it was her *duty* to do so. Sexual enjoyment was for a wanton woman only; it was not something a *lady* experienced.

Then Sigmund Freud came along. Dr. Freud said it was OK for women to enjoy sex. But *orgasm* for women was a luxury at this point, because her man would usually reach a climax too soon. It was her duty to accept this, and not to make demands on her husband. She was conditioned to keep quiet about her needs.

It was not until 1966 that Dr. William Masters and Mrs. Virginia Johnson cast aside, once and for all, the idea that an orgasm for a woman was a luxury. What's more, they proved that, if properly stimulated, a woman can achieve one or more orgasms for each act of sexual intercourse—and that she has the potential for many more. Perhaps equally important, Masters and Johnson's world famous report, *Human Sexual Response,* gave new insights on how couples could help themselves and each other to achieve more complete orgasmic release.

I firmly believe that the orgasm can help a woman to become more *beautiful all over*—from the hair on her head to the nails on her toes. The following chapter will explain in detail exactly how this beautifying process takes place. But first, in case there is any doubt in your mind, I'd like to clear up any misinformation you may have about orgasms, and their being really necessary for your beauty and mental and physical health.

Did you ever hear the story of the ugly duckling who married and blossomed into a beautiful, graceful swan? If you thought that it was just coincidence, it's not. Orgasm is a natural, normal, and healthy bodily response. Wilhelm Reich, in his book *Function of the Orgasm,* describes it like this: "Orgastic potency is the capacity to surrender to the flow of biological energy, free of any inhibitions; the capacity to discharge completely the damned-up sexual excitation through involuntary, pleasurable convulsions of the body." In layman's language orgasm may be defined as the moment of release of built-up sexual tension—sexual tension which builds up in women just as it does in men.

To be clinical about it, there is definite evidence that animals suffer from sexual abstinence. Research has shown that in laboratory rats regular mating leads to greater longevity, and increases resistance to chemical and biological poisons, infections, and strain. It was also found that in some animals sexual intercourse is necessary for the optimal functioning of the endocrine system. (In various parts of the body there are a number of important glands that form the endocrine system. They secrete hormones, which are chemical substances required for the chemical regulation of the body, some hormones actually being essential for life itself.) Most animals who are forced to abstain over long periods of time tend to show symptoms very much like human anxiety.

We now know that tension and anxiety in human beings inevitably leads to depression, lethargy, and often insomnia. But its physical results are even more insidious, because tension can wreak havoc on the glandular system, subjecting one to the dangers of heart ailments, kidney dysfunction, high blood pressure, diabetes, arthritis, allergies, and more.

If all this doesn't convince you that orgasms are the best kind of "preventive medicine" available, read on!

18

The Orgasm as a Beautifier— It Will Help You Stay 29 Forever

ORGASM IS A total physical response to the pleasure of lovemaking. In a very short span of time, a woman's body undergoes dramatic changes that are believed to make a large contribution to overall physical beauty. Indeed, sexual hormones circulate to every part of her body from head to toe. Here's how it happens.

Dr. Masters and Mrs. Johnson have defined orgasm in four stages: 1) Excitement Phase; 2) Plateau Phase; 3) Orgasm; 4) Resolution Phase. These four stages have a very definite effect on every part of a woman's body.

Before sexual excitement the sexual organs are in a resting state. As a woman becomes sexually aroused through any form of stimulation, the Excitement Phase begins. Remember that an orgasm for beauty can be obtained with a partner or be self-induced. Emotionally there may be a difference, but for beauty purposes, it doesn't matter whether it occurs during intercourse, masturbation, or any other form of stimulation. Doctors have long used "therapeutic masturbation" to help a female overcome what is called "orgasm impairment." In all cases the climax is the same.

As the Excitement Phase begins, blood starts to accumulate in the pelvic area and sexual organs. One of the first signs of sexual excitement in a woman is the presence of vaginal lubrication which comes from the walls of the vagina and is caused by a rise in the vaginal temperature.

As sexual excitement continues, the vagina expands and lengthens, and as blood accumulates in the pelvic area, the vaginal tissues begin to swell, along with the clitoris and breasts. The nipples, sometimes at this point, begin to become erect. Also, during the build-up stage to orgasm, the muscles of a woman's arms and legs, thighs and buttocks contract, and most often she will also tense up the muscles in her abdomen as she tilts her pelvis up towards her mate. (This latter response is a learned response in some women, natural in others.) Probably her facial muscles are tensing up, too. All this, with special emphasis being given to such problem areas such as the buttocks, abdomen and inner thighs, is very much like a beautifully coordinated isometrics exercise.

As sexual excitement continues to build, the Plateau Phase (phase 2) is reached. The outer lips of the vagina become more swollen as the orgasm approaches. The tissues of the walls of the outer third of the vagina—including the PC muscle (that's short for the pubococcygeal muscle, the muscle controlling the first third of the vagina)—swell with blood and the vaginal opening becomes more narrow.

As sexual excitement mounts, the heart pumps blood faster and faster, breathing speeds up, and so does the pulse rate. A normal heart beats at an average rate of seventy-two beats a minute, but during orgasm it may escalate to an astonishing three beats a second! Breathing goes from a normal sixteen to eighteen breaths a minute to nearly fifty. Many women also experience what doctors usually refer to as the sexual flush—a blushlike color over the skin of the face, neck, and chest, as more blood and heat rises to the body's surface, and blood continues to accumulate in the pelvic area. At this point a film of perspiration can appear over some women's bodies.

This revving-up of circulation is much like the by-product of very effective physical exercise. But no other "exercise" is as natural as this or affects as many parts of the body at the same time; it delivers the greatest number of beauty and health benefits.

As stimulation is continued, the woman moves into the Orgasmic Phase (phase 3). Breathing, pulse rate, and blood pressure continue to rise. Breathing becomes faster. The increased muscle tension and increased blood supply to the sexual tissues reach a peak. Then suddenly the PC muscle contracts rhythmically for a brief period. (The contractions vary depending on the strength of the orgasm.) The muscles of the uterus and abdominal area contract, as does the hand and foot reflex, with a grasping muscular response. With the completion of the orgasm, everything—breathing, circulation, etc.—begins to return to normal.

Now the Resolution Phase (phase 4) begins. The sexual organs return to the resting position. The vagina shrinks back to its normal size within a few minutes to half an hour after orgasm. If orgasm has not occurred, the resolution phase can take one or two hours.

But the female body is as unique as it is complex, because a woman is quite capable, immediately after completing one orgasm, of moving directly into another—or into a whole series of orgasms, one after another. She is capable of multiple orgasms if she can keep her sexual excitement above the level of the Plateau Phase (phase 2) at which she started her climax.

A woman can also extend the length of time of each orgasm much longer than a man. The male climax usually lasts only a few seconds, while a woman can experience a series of rapidly recurring orgasms with no decrease in sexual excitement until the very end. Her orgasmic period can vary from a few seconds to more than a minute.

Altogether it's quite an extraordinary performance. It's why so many women appear to glow with fresh new beauty when they're in love and enjoying a healthy sexual relationship. Orgasm helps you to achieve your highest level of individual beauty as it affects every part of your body, inside and out. Your complexion appears more youthfully radiant, your muscle tone improves, even your hair looks shinier and more bouncy. Happily this can happen at *any* age!

Furthermore, Beauty-Orgasms can keep you feeling young no matter how many birthdays you've celebrated. One of the great European "youth doctors," who has pioneered certain well-known rejuvenation techniques, states that "the most powerful tonic is orgasm; it is the secret of youthful expression."

19

The Psychological
Approach
to the Beauty-Orgasm

BEFORE WE GET into the actual beauty treatments,
let's take a look at some of the psychological aspects
of orgasm. I consider this to be of utmost
importance, because you can derive many more
beauty and health benefits from sex if you can put
yourself into the proper frame of mind.

In this context two questions come to mind: (1)
Why are men more orgasmic than women? (2) What
can women do—psychologically—to improve their
capacity for orgasm? Perhaps the most important
reason the male is more orgasmic is that sex is of
great importance to him. Because of this, a man
frequently thinks about, fantasizes about, day-
dreams about making love. Maybe he mentally
reviews his last, or most satisfying sexual encounter.
Perhaps he recreates the body of the woman he
loves in his mind. Maybe he mentally acts out his
most thrilling sexual fantasy. But whatever he
chooses to think about, a man will play these

fantasy "tapes" over and over in his mind, spending a great deal of time in this imaginary sexual activity. Since sex is so frequently on his mind, he is more "psyched up" to create and enjoy sexual encounters at any time they may present themselves.

We women can learn a great deal from this. All the physical stimulation in the world cannot produce an orgasm if desire or attention is absent. If your mind is elsewhere, or if you are angry or too tense, or worried, your *mind* will block your body from experiencing orgasm. (Interruptions during lovemaking also can lower the level of arousal.)

Feeling sexual comes directly from *thinking* sexually. A high state of mental sexual arousal is most important to orgasm release. You can *train* yourself to be more erotically responsive by using what I like to call "Mental Aphrodisiacs." These stimulants vary from "replaying" your last pleasurable lovemaking session over in your mind, to reading an erotic novel (perhaps a classic like *Fanny Hill*), or indulging in imaginative, original sexual fantasies.

Remember, fantasies are *perfectly normal*. Just because you fantasize about a certain thing does not mean that you actually want to act it out. The best fantasies of all are those that never get acted out; acting them out would only ruin their "fantastical" quality, and rob them of erotic stimulation. Keeping fantasies as just mental stimulation, and using them as a tool to explore your own personal erotic level, can make them one of the most valuable aids to more enjoyable lovemaking.

Once you have mastered the art of fantasizing, you can then train your mind to fantasize at will.

Just imagine what would happen to your mental arousal level if you were able to "command" your mind to think of something sensual at any time or any place. We spend a great deal of time and money studying makeup, hair, fashion, diet, and beauty in general in order to make us appealing to the opposite sex on the *outside*. Why not spend at least part of that time training your mind to function in a way that will increase your "inner" sexuality, which, in turn, leads to the kind of love life that will naturally make you look more radiantly beautiful! Remember, the more you mentally plan for love, the more you will enjoy it, and that means the more total beauty for you.

Now let's get back to the point I made about "commanding" your mind to think about sex. Here are some specific ways to do it:

First of all, start by setting aside a little time each day to occupy your mind with sexual thoughts: perhaps after you've got your husband and the children off to work and school, and you're finally alone in the house, and free from interruption. (If this all sounds a little mechanical to you, don't worry. Your mind will soon take over and you'll be doing it automatically.)

If you're still stumped about exactly what to think about, try this one at the beginning: imagine that your man is making love to you with all the passionate freedom in the world, completely without hangups—yours or his. Go over this fantasy slowly in your mind, savoring each emotion and sensation separately and completely. Then when you've completed that scene, reverse the procedure and fantasize that *you're* the aggressor, making love to your lover in a way that will give you the most pleasure imaginable. Again, run this through your mind slowly, perhaps "replaying" the most exciting parts as many times as you like. Men do this all the time. Soon you won't need help—your imagination will take over and create lovely and stimulating fantasies all by itself!

Remember, the more you fantasize, the more you will want to make love, and the more ready you will be to relax and enjoy it. If you've got sexual hangups (and everybody has at least one or two!) fantasizing will help you to get rid of them. Plus, if you fantasize regularly, it will help to break down any resistance you may have about discussing your sexual hangups with your man. As with everything else, more communication in sex inevitably leads to more understanding of both your needs and those of your man, and, ultimately of course, to greater mutual enjoyment of your sexual relationship.

If you're still finding difficulty in fantasizing, here are a few pointers that might make it easier:

1) Think about the last time your man really pleased you sexually. Go over it detail by detail. Then think about the last time he really enjoyed your lovemaking.

2) If you are confused about any aspect of the sex act, read a book or two on the subject. There are plenty of worthwhile ones on the market that will clear up any questions you may have about your own sexual feelings or ability. For instance, you might like to read: *For Yourself* by Lonnie Garfield Barbach (Doubleday, 1975); *How to Get More out of Sex* (Bantam, 1975) or *Any Woman Can!* by Dr. David Reuben (Bantam, 1972); *Human Sexual*

Response by Dr. William Masters and Mrs. Virginia Johnson (Little Brown, 1966).

3) Mentally go back to your honeymoon—or the first year you were married—and recreate that lovemaking. Again, go over it slowly, savoring each and every detail. (If you can't remember all the details, make some up to fill in the blanks.)

4) The skin is a sexual organ—2,800 inches of it. Make use of this primary sexual organ to open up more orgasmic possibilities. Relearn your most erotic zones; ask your partner to help you to find them. Maybe it's your inner thighs, abdomen, upper arms, back, or even the nape of your neck. While this is happening, think your most pleasurable thoughts.

5) Get used to thinking of your body as a vehicle for exquisite pleasure, something that can give you a great deal of enjoyment. Think over and over that you deserve the kind of pleasure your body can give and receive. Know that the Bible approves of sex and has told woman to give her body to her husband, and her husband to give his to his wife. This should help to rid you of any lingering hangups or anxieties about sexual pleasure. Think about your lover's body. Mentally go over it slowly. Imagine all the good feelings that you get from each part of his body.

6) Start thinking about things you can use to create an erotic and romantic mood for your next sexual encounter, for instance bath oil, bubble bath, a new scent, or sensual nightgown, anything that makes you feel especially alluring. Then go out and buy these things if you don't already have them.

Whoever said that the mind was the first sexual

organ sure knew what he (or she) was talking about. Because the mind holds the key to erotic enjoyment, it can be used to open up a whole new world of sexual pleasure for you and your partner. All it takes is a little mental discipline in the beginning. Before you know it, it will all become so natural that you'll wonder why you never "thought" of it before!

20

Before-Orgasm Beauty Treatments

POSSIBLY THE MOST important thing about being 29 Forever is that you always feel beautiful, and feeling beautiful is the most important part of *being* beautiful. If you feel beautiful, your eyes sparkle and your face acquires a perpetually "up," happy look. You seem to glow all over.

How do you think women who are actually not beautiful make you think they are beautiful? Take a close look at the attractive women you see on your TV screen. Many of them are not half as beautiful as they seem. It's just that they have acquired the knack of making you think they are. Because they've learned to treat themselves so beautifully, they become convinced that they are beautiful—and that convinces you!

The 29 Forever woman knows that beauty starts with a firm belief in herself, a belief that says "*I* can look beautiful." You've surely learned by now that every woman can if she has the will to do so. You have to spend time, thought, and money on hair care, makeup, exercise, and various dieting regimens, but it can't stop there. You must continue on to realize your full beauty potential with Beauty-Orgasms.

Try the following simple before-beauty-orgasm treatments: a special bath that I take when I'm not feeling particularly beautiful, the sensuous and beautifying body massage, and some special exercises that will help you to achieve many more Beauty-Orgasms.

My Special Bath Recipe

My own personal tub bath is the most erotic nonsexual experience I can think of, and I'd like to pass it along to you. It's guaranteed to make you feel T-E-R-R-I-F-I-C—all over!

1) Fill your tub with warm water but not too hot—hot water can make you overfatigued, and thus act as a sexual deterrent. Add your favorite bubble bath or bath oil now.

2) Add one or two drops (only) of your sexiest perfume or cologne.

3) Prepare a long, cool glass of your favorite drink. I sometimes prefer a glass of chilled white wine, or one-half glass of cold milk. (No coffee! It provides a momentary lift, but what goes up must come down. The down side has the effect of a slight "withdrawal" reaction, which is certainly not conducive to sexual desire.) Set the drink on the

edge of the tub, or any place else within easy reach.

4) Take the phone off the hook, unless you can appoint someone else to answer it and take messages. It's important that you have *absolutely no interruptions* during this time. If you find it soothing, put on some music.

5) Tie your hair up (no ugly bath cap) in a glamourous way. How you look is how you feel.

6) Now *slowly* sink back into the tub up to your shoulders. R-E-L-A-X. Do nothing for five minutes except to slowly sip your drink.

7) After you are completely relaxed, soap a washcloth and stand up and wash your body. Throw the soapy washcloth into the *sink* after you're through—not back into the tub—keeping the bath water as fresh as possible. Once again, sink back into the tub. Sip your drink. Don't get out of the bath until you feel completely relaxed.

8) Step out and dry yourself off with a large bath towel. (Or maybe you should let your lover dry you.) Gently rub your body all over with a scented body lotion. Now sit, or lie, down for a few moments and just savor the sense of relaxation that has taken hold of you.

The Massage

Sensual massage is one *terrific* way to become aware of the body once again. The aim of sensual massage is to induce, slowly and naturally, a relaxed physical contentment so that two people can make love in a state of close physical trust and harmony. Gentle, sensual massaging of a partner's body can gradually become more erotic, leading to sexual excitement for both partners. Massage, however, need not always be a prelude to sexual intercourse; rather, it can be used as a "sensuality exercise" designed to sharpen awareness of the body, and finely tune all the physical perceptions.

The sensual massage is very gentle, slow, and rhythmic; you never hurt your partner, or make sudden movements. It's a marvelous way for two lovers who already know each other well to deepen their physical relationship; or for an inhibited partner to learn how to relax; or for two people who do not know each other very intimately to start trusting.

A good time for sensual massage is any time you and your lover are sure to be undisturbed. Start with a bath, using scented foam or oil and a natural sponge. Soap each part of your partner's body gently, moving over the entire body, then rinsing with warm water. Now pat him dry with a soft, heated towel. Don't rush this part!

Set the scene for the massage by clearing the room of any outside distractions such as noise or bright light. Ask your partner to lie on his stomach on the bed, or better still on a thick rug or towel on the floor. For the ultimate sensual experience, use a fur rug or spread a satin sheet over the surface of the place where you're going to give the massage. Do not speak during the massage; let your bodies do the talking.

The ideal background is silence, which allows the person you are massaging to concentrate completely on the physical sensations, but there is no reason why you should not have music if you prefer. There should be just enough light to allow you to see what you're doing—try candlelight. Do not wear any clothes while you're massaging because that immediately puts a barrier between you and your partner.

To begin, kneel down beside your partner. Spread your hands and the area to be massaged with a fine mineral oil, which you can buy at the drugstore. Baby oil is just as good. Warm up the oil in the palm of your hand before applying to the body.

Keep in mind that you're trying to induce a state of relaxed physical well-being, rather than sexual excitement, during the massage. *That* part can come later. Do each movement three times—unless your partner really likes it, in which case stay with it. Work very slowly and rhythmically, using your whole body, not just your arms and hands.

Begin with the back of the neck; this area is usually a tension-magnet. Using your fingers, work up and down the sides of the neck from the base of the skull to the shoulder bones. Then move to the center of the neck and, using the forefinger and thumb of one hand, make small circular movements, again moving from the base of the skull to the shoulders.

When you are finished, slide your hands down to the shoulders and back area. You should spend about half your total time on the back because it's here that you'll do the most good. Back massage increases the blood supply to the spine and the nerves of the upper body. Use both circular and long stroking movements. Go over the small of the back with special care because massage here often creates sexual excitement in the male. You can use this feeling to give added pleasure to your massage as well as to build up anticipation for what will come after.

Begin massaging the back with long strokes from the base of the neck to the lower back, using the whole weight of your body. Continuing these deep, stroking movements, move very slowly up and then down the back; then begin to alternate with small, circular movements. Make small, quick movements with your fingers up and down the spine, or draw crisscross zigzags with your thumbs, quickly and lightly.

If your partner is excessively tense (and by this time he shouldn't be) there may still be areas of knotted muscle around the base of the neck. To loosen them up, knead the whole area with your knuckles or fingertips. (Be especially careful when using your fingertips that you don't scratch the skin with your nails!)

Move on to the arms, using long, stroking movements from shoulder to wrist. Lift the arm slightly so that your hands move around all sides. Shake it gently to eliminate any tension. Gradually work down to the fingertips, gently massaging the palms and pulling gently on the fingers.

Now move to the legs and feet. Work on one leg at a time with both hands. Duplicating the long, stroking movements that you used on the arms, massage the calf, thigh, and once again, the calf. (Do not massage the knee area; pressure on this sensitive joint may prove harmful.) Then rest one of your partner's feet on your thigh as you stroke the foot smoothly up and down its length, over the top and underneath, working around the ankle bones with circular movements of the thumbs. Finish with the toes, massaging each one separately.

Now return to the back and once again stroke the body with long, flowing movements, moving from the base of the neck down to the top of the buttocks. Use this technique for a few minutes, then ask your partner to turn over on his back.

Begin this side of the body with a facial massage, very gently running your fingertips over the cheeks and temples from the chin to the hairline. Using the very tips of your fingers, make small, circular movements around the eyes and on to the temples. Finish off with soft, stroking movements across the forehead from side to side, running your fingers into the hairline.

Now move down to the shoulders and chest. Move lightly down the chest with firm, long movements. Massage the shoulders with circular movements of the heel of your hand, then smooth them with long strokes, gradually coming down over the chest again. Continue the stroking movements over the midriff and stomach, firmly but gently. (Never press hard on the stomach area. This may cause damage to the internal organs.)

Move to the arms and the legs, massaging them in the same way as you did from the back. To finish up, cover the entire body with long, soft, stroking movements. Gradually lightening the pressure, slow down. Then quietly and gently break contact with your partner's body.

Special Exercises to Help You
Achieve Your Beauty-Orgasm

Years ago someone with a decided flair for publicity referred to lovemaking as "man's favorite indoor sport." I take exception to that. Why confine it to the masculine gender?

Yet the demands that sexual intercourse make upon the body of a man and the body of a woman do differ, and greatly, too. So I strongly recommend that, in order to get maximum pleasure from Beauty-Orgasm, you exercise those parts of your anatomy that play the principal parts in lovemaking. For developing your sexual prowess is, I think, very much like developing physical prowess in any sport.

As we previously mentioned, the large muscle that surrounds the opening of the vagina is called the *pubococcygeal* muscle, or PC muscle as it's more commonly known, and it contracts during orgasm. Like any muscle, the better toned it is, the better it performs. The following exercises have been specially created to give this muscle the exercise it needs to perform its very best.

Before you begin these exercises, however, I suggest you decide for yourself how effectively your PC muscle is working at present. This is very simple to do: just lie down and insert your middle finger in the opening of your vagina and contract this muscle. Ideally it should contract to the point where it squeezes around your finger.

The following exercises will keep the PC muscle in this prime condition, or if the muscle is lacking in tone (and this is the case with the majority of women, particularly those who have given birth), then these exercises will help remedy that condition. Either way, these exercises—in fact, *all* the exercises in this chapter—should be done daily for as long as you wish to remain sexually active. That means, I hope, that you will do them faithfully for the rest of your life.

1) This first exercise is very basic and can be done anywhere, at any time. You contract your PC muscle, hold it that way to the count of three, and then relax it. Some women will find this easier to do than others. If you should find that you can't hold the contraction to the count of three, then hold it to the count of two. Either way, be certain to do a series of ten contractions *three times each day*. Then the easier it becomes for you to do them, the more repetitions you do, until you're holding each contraction to the full count of six. It doesn't matter where you do this exercise because only you will know that you're doing it. The main thing is that you do it *every day, three times a day*.

2) Once you've gotten the knack of exercise number one, add this exercise; like the previous one, it can be done anywhere, at any time. It's simply the next very logical step in toning up your very important PC muscle. You contract the muscle, but instead of holding the contraction, you release it quickly and then—just as quickly—squeeze again and release again. It's One-Two...One-Two; as quickly as possible. Again, this is a ten-repetition exercise to be done *every day, three times a day*.

3) This is your final PC muscle exercise and it simply builds on the expertise you've acquired doing the first two. I find lying down is the best

position for this exercise, but it isn't essential that you lie down. (Like the two previous exercises, this too can be done anywhere, at any time.) This exercise can be done in or out of water, but I find that it is particularly effective when done in a tub where the vagina can work against the pressure of the water and, as a result, you can more readily feel your PC muscle working. Imagine an egg is placed between your thighs, just outside the opening to your vagina. Attempt to draw that imaginary egg up into your vagina. When you feel you've taken it in, hold it there to the count of three by contracting your PC muscle. Then, pressing down hard, eject it to the count of three. That is, control the release of this imaginary egg so that it leaves the vagina in three stages. Repeat this exercise ten times. Like the two previous exercises, it should be done *every day, three times a day*.

The three exercises above concentrate on the vagina. But as we've already noted, sexual intercourse involves much more than one part of your anatomy. It's the uninhibited ease and expertise with which you use all these parts that make it possible for you to experience a Beauty-Orgasm. Now here are some exercises designed to benefit the pelvic area and make you feel freer sexually. But before I describe them, let me take time out to tell you about the fascinating Scandinavian woman who taught them to me.

Her name was Love. I met her when I was new to New York, and we became fast friends. To this day I don't know if "Love" was her given name, or if she simply adopted it. It doesn't matter. It fit her perfectly; she was always in love.

Love was a lemon-blonde, tiny and exquisitely proportioned. She looked no more than a ravishing thirty-five, but one evening she confided to me that she was fifty-seven. She credited her youthful face and figure to a slimming diet, proper exercise—and a very active, very happy love life. "Be in love always, Oleda," she counseled me. "It may cause acne in the very young, but it brings nothing but smiles to older women." (You see now why I questioned the origin of her name?)

One evening some weeks later, Love asked me if I'd like to see some exercises she said were designed to benefit the pelvic area and make you feel freer sexually. Of course I said yes, and she promptly sank to her knees on the floor of her studio and proceeded to demonstrate the following exercises. Not only will they teach you how to strengthen and control your pelvis, but they will also, as an added bonus, firm your thighs and buttocks at the same time.

1) Kneel with knees and feet together. Relax and place your hands on your hips. Then tilt back so that your pelvis is thrust forward. Now move your pelvis—smoothly, loosely—first to the left, then to the right. Do this ten times. Once you feel confident that you have control, begin to slowly make circles with your pelvis. (I suggest you do this exercise to music. I prefer fast or rock music, but you might like belly-dance music. Whichever music you choose, I think you'll find that it will tend to make you less inhibited.)

2) In a kneeling position with knees together, sit back on your feet and stretch both arms high above your head. Now raise your derrière off your

feet about two inches. Tighten buttocks and then tilt pelvis forward. Maintain this position for the count of ten. Next, return pelvis—slowly, smoothly—to its so-called "normal" position, while arching your back slowly. (This is a serpentine motion and should be slow and sensuous. Don't rush.) Do this pelvic movement a total of six times, then sit back on your feet and lower your arms to your sides and relax. Do three repetitions.

3) Assume kneeling position with feet and knees together. (It's important that your back be perfectly straight throughout this exercise.) Place palms flat against your thighs. Now lean backward ever so slowly. Go back as far as you can go with your back still perfectly straight, hold still, and raise both arms slowly above your head. Hold this position for a slow count of six. Return to starting position, making your thigh muscles work to pull you up. Do three repetitions.

Love? Unhappily I lost track of her. She returned to Scandinavia some years ago. But I feel certain that she's happy, healthy, and in love as always. She'll be 29 Forever!

21

Beauty Benefits During Orgasm

THE BEAUTY BENEFITS during lovemaking and orgasm seem endless. There is just no other activity that will give you more overall beauty.

During the sex act the glands are stimulated. In the sexually excited person, the pituitary gland pours hormones into the bloodstream, triggering reactions in the adrenals and gonads, or sex organs. In this complex chain reaction of the endocrine system, the gonads secrete sex hormones necessary for sexual drive and are involved in the regulation of your general health.

Before we go any further, let me say that the endocrine system (see illustrations) is a group of glands that secrete into the bloodstream one or more specific chemical compounds known as hormones. Hormones are chemical messengers that arouse or set into motion certain functions necessary for the body as a whole. These hormones are carried to virtually every part of the body, reaching the various organs and tissues that will affect your health and beauty.

The endocrine glands play a very large part in your overall beauty. In every individual they significantly affect the activity of every cell in the body. They influence mental acuity, physical agility, build and stature, bodily hair growth, voice pitch, sexual urge, and behavior. The endocrine system tempers every waking and sleeping moment of life and constantly modifies the way we feel, think, behave, and react to all sorts of stimuli.

Obviously sex is good for you—in more ways than one. Orgasm feeds every part of your body, therefore providing both direct and indirect beauty. Yet in our society today, there are many women conditioned to ignore this aspect of life. We must remember that not only is sex a God-given pleasure, but it is necessary to the full completion of a woman's personality and femininity. Sex is a necessary biological function, and orgasm is not only very pleasurable, but is a vital part of good health—and beauty.

If a woman experiences the excitement and tension of sexual activity without an orgasm, the effect upon her body is often harmful. Sexual frustrations caused by abstinence or lack of orgasm put a powerful strain on the mind and body. If this condition persists, it can lead to many physical and emotional disturbances.

Masters and Johnson have confirmed that abstaining from sex does not only affect the area of the sex organs. They found that it does indeed involve the circulatory, respiratory, glandular, and muscle systems of the entire body—male or female.

A nonorgasmic woman is being deprived of many benefits such as release of energy, better relaxation, and true zest for living. Unlike the temporary draining effect it has on the man, sex normally serves to enhance a woman's beauty, restore her vitality, and make her feel years younger.

1   The Pituitary Gland

The pituitary gland is called the "master sex gland" because its hormones dictate to all the other sex glands. (Removal of the pituitary gland is followed by atrophy of the sex glands.) It produces several hormones which enter the bloodstream and stimulate the other sex glands. It is also called the "mental" sex gland, because if it is not stimulated first, the other sex glands will not start to work.

The pituitary sends out different hormones to different sex glands with this message: "Get ready—fill up with your own hormones." (They do just that, if you have allowed the message to be completed.) Once these sex glands are filled with their own hormones each of these glands sends a message to the pituitary gland saying, "Stop stimulating us—we don't need your help anymore." They don't, for now the "physical" sex glands (marked 2 through 7) have taken over.

2   The Thyroid Gland

This gland changes iodine into compounds of great hormonal activity. After the body digests food with iodine, the circulation—or bloodstream—is responsible for carrying the iodine up to the thyroid. The iodine is then converted into a hormone called Thyroglobulin, which is stored in sufficient quantities in the thyroid. By the time this hormone is actually released, it's called *Thyroxine*. Upon its release, it travels to every tissue and cell in the body, stimulating them by producing heat and using up oxygen. Only small amounts of iodine are needed by the body, but these amounts are essential.

Our diet becomes deficient in iodine when there is little or no iodine in the soil where the food we buy is grown. Parts of America are known to have little or no iodine.

Foods providing iodine are sea fish, shell fish, water, vegetables grown where soil contains iodine, and iodized salt. (See page 154.)

Although very often the lack of iodine is responsible for a thyroid problem, there may be other reasons. Malfunctioning of the pituitary gland or the inability of the thyroid to retain the hormone are some of the other reasons. See your doctor if you suspect these problems.

3 The Parathyroid Glands

The four parathyroid glands are imbedded in the thyroid glands. They produce two hormones called "parathormone" and "calcitonen." Their main function is to maintain your calcium and phosphorus level of the blood. (If removed, death due to convulsion would occur.) Very low calcium levels in the blood causes twitching, cramps, and spasms of the hands and feet. It can also cause muscular weakness, cataracts, constipation, blood clotting, nervous activity, and softening of the bones, which then are prone to fracture. None of these conditions, needless to say, adds to one's overall beauty.

Besides calcium and phosphorus, these glands also produce other minerals, such as potassium, magnesium, manganese, all of which are necessary to maintain our beauty and good health.

Keeping a close check on your diet so that you achieve the proper balance, and adding more Vitamin D to it, can help your parathyroid gland to do a better job for you. Oral calcium and other minerals can be taken. However, this must be done under a doctor's care, since too much of these minerals can do you more harm than good.

4 The Thymus Gland

This gland helps provide resistance to disease and infections. It helps maintain muscle function and produces lymphocytes. If this gland is not functioning properly, muscles tend to become abnormally fatigued.

5 The Adrenal Glands

These two glands lie on the top of each kidney, and both of them play important roles in maintaining health and combating disease. Each gland is made up of two types of tissues: cortex and medulla. The medulla lies inside the cortex, but each secretes different hormones and functions quite independ-

1. Pituitary Gland

2. Thyroid Gland

3. Four Parathyroid Glands
   (Imbedded in the Thyroid Gland)

4. Thymus Gland

5. Adrenal Gland

6. Pancreas Gland

7. Ovary Glands

The Endocrine System

These are all ductless sex glands. The hormones secreted from them go directly into the bloodstream to begin the beautifying process.

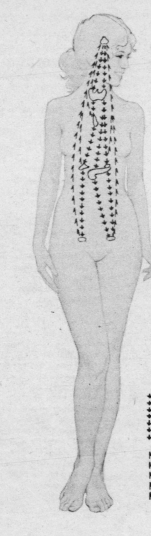

The Action of the Endocrine System

Message from the pituitary to all other sex glands to go into action.

Shut-off message sent back to the pituitary gland by *each* sex gland.

The Apocrine System

There are two million of these tiny glands, which excrete fluids known as preporatin or "fat droplets" through ducts (or tubes). These glands are not considered "sex" glands—*but they are beauty glands.*

The two types of Apocrine Sweat Glands are:

1. *Apocrine sweat glands*—These open into hair follicles and are limited to fewer regions of the body, the underarm and genital areas. Apocrine sweat contains complex substances that give it a milky appearance.

2. *Eccrine sweat glands*—Many thousands of these glands are present almost *everywhere* under the skin. Each of these glands has a duct that leads to the skin surface. These glands form fat droplets which, mixed up with castoff cell materials and debris, are called "skin oil." Then this "skin oil" seeps through a duct into a hair follicle, lubricates this hairy shaft, then goes on to the skin surface to lubricate.

ently. The difference between the two parts will be explained below.

The Adrenal Cortex: The cortex is essential to life. (The medulla is not.) Total destruction of the cortex leads to rapid death.

Several hormones are produced by this part of the gland, but the three main ones are:

a) *Gluccocorticoids*—These are cortisonelike substances that influence carbohydrate, protein, and fat metabolism.

b) *Mineralocorticoids*—Regulate water and salt balance.

c) *Sex steroids*—Act as an auxiliary source of sex hormones.

These hormones (A, B, & C) regulate many aspects of our body functions and if anything goes wrong with this gland, serious disturbances will occur. These disturbances affect your beauty directly or indirectly. It can cause you to put on too much weight, and could also cause you to lose too much. In addition, it can directly change your sexual function. It can also cause low blood pressure, pigmentation of the skin, and loss of sexual hair. All this can be corrected with the help of a doctor.

The Adrenal Medulla: This is the inner portion of the adrenal gland. It is intimately connected with the sympathetic nervous system. The medulla produces two hormones called adrenaline and noradrenaline.

The value of our adrenal glands really comes into play in cases where we are forced to experience excessive stress, trauma, tension, or overwork. We depend on the ability of our pituitary gland to respond to such situations by secreting adequate amounts of ACTH (a hormone produced by the anterior part of the pituitary gland) to stimulate the adrenal gland. This stimulation results in what is now termed the "flight or fight" response: a surge of quick energy, increased muscular strength, dilated pupils (for better sight), and contraction of the blood vessels.

But once these energies are used up, they must be replenished if you are not to feel completely depleted. So the adrenalin hormones stimulate the pituitary gland to produce more ACTH hormone, which stimulates the adrenal cortex. When this happens, a cortisonelike hormone is released to induce the conversion of glucose from proteins and replenish the sugar in the liver and muscles that was used up in the "alarm" reaction.

(With the aid of cortisonelike substances administered by a doctor, regulated salt intake, and adherence to a well-balanced diet, most people who frequently experience this excessive "stress" reaction can be kept in good health.)

6   The Pancreas Gland

The pancreas gland secretes insulin hormone as well as digestive enzymes.

The pancreas is a double-purpose gland. It secretes insulin hormone into the blood, not into the digestive tract. Insulin is concerned with the *utilization* of sugar. Entirely different pancreas cells produce clear, watery pancreatic juice, which contains enzymes that split fats, proteins, and carbohydrates. (If a failing pancreas is in an acute stage, diabetes results.)

7   The Ovary Glands

The ovaries have two functions: 1) provide egg cells; 2) secrete hormones. They secrete two hormones: estrogen and progesterone.

The ovaries are regulated by the pituitary gland. Without their production of hormones, premature signs of aging appear. These hormones also help to regulate the function of the uterus. Lack of them can also cause early arthritis in menopause.

The Beauty Benefits

All the glands just discussed have a direct relationship to your beauty. Listed below are the beauty benefits related to these glands and orgasm. The beauty "treatment" for each one listed can come from one or more of these seven sex glands.

The surface of your skin: Arteries and veins in the pelvic area constrict because during orgasm the small muscles controlling the size of the blood vessels contract involuntarily. Many women experience a warm feeling over the surface of the entire body as these small blood vessels of the skin relax, and bring more blood and heat to the surface of the body. The skin may even turn a flushed, reddish color. This process is an excellent skin treatment because it promotes good circulation in the skin's outer layer and carries oil and moisture to the pores (even though you can't see it). This results in the skin's acquiring a youthful, healthy glow. Moisture is also retained in the pores, preventing more rapid aging and leaving the surface of the skin soft, silky, and sensuous to the touch.

Deep breathing: During orgasms the rate of breathing becomes faster and deeper. The breathing rate, normally sixteen to eighteen breaths per minute at rest, may leap to near fifty at orgasm—a rate comparable to the most strenuous exercise. As the respiratory rate soars and excessive breathing becomes extremely deep and rapid, hyperventilation usually occurs. More oxygen is being brought into the body and the lungs are being used to their fullest capacity. Also, dangerous toxins are removed from the body with each deep exhalation.

Heart: Orgasm speeds up the circulation, which affects flow of blood, which in turn, affects the heartbeat. The pulse rate, an average seventy-two beats per minute at rest, accelerates to as high as 180 beats per minute at climax. So, during sexual activity, the heart gets more of a workout than during many other forms of exercise, such as jogging. But there is no indication that such strenuous exertion taken in moderation will harm a healthy heart. On the contrary, there is strong evidence that regular exercise is good insurance against a possible heart attack. In fact, sex is one form of strenuous exercise highly beneficial to the heart and circulatory system, and body muscles as well.

Eyes: During orgasm the iris contracts. The orgasm also provides isometric exercise for the tiny muscles around the eyes. For instance, it exercises the muscle that prevents upper and lower eyelid drop and puffy skin at inside corners of the eye. The muscle that controls eye opening is also involved, and this helps to smooth out the crow's feet area of the eyes. The increased circulation helps to keep eyes clear and bright, and helps to prevent puffiness around the eyes.

Hair: During the buildup of sexual excitement and orgasm, the accelerated heart rate pumping blood throughout the body at a much faster speed rushes the blood to the roots of the hair, feeding and nourishing them. If your head is lying flat on the bed—rather than propped up on a pillow or sitting up—your roots will benefit from an additional flow of blood. Good circulation to the face and head is very important for healthy hair because it gives stronger hair shaft (roots), which prevents abnormal falling out; it promotes faster growth of lustrous, shining hair; and it helps prevent brittle hair and split ends.

Nails: These also receive several benefits from the Beauty Orgasm: faster growth, a stronger, smoother surface, less breakage and splitting.

General body condition is enhanced in the following ways:

... It's easier to maintain your correct weight

... Your mental and physical energy levels are increased

... Your limbs are more supple and limber

The Beauty Orgasm as Exercise

The Beauty Orgasm yields many of the same benefits as does a conventional (and boring) exercise regimen. For instance, muscles in the arms, legs, abdomen, neck, and face begin to tense when climax is imminent. Although this movement is voluntary at first, it becomes involuntary as orgasm approaches.

Arms: During orgasm the muscles in your arms contract involuntarily, which helps to keep your arms taut and youthful looking. Nothing can look more aging on a young woman than saggy flesh on her upper arms. These involuntary exercises are much easier (and more fun) than calisthenics.

Legs: The leg muscles also contract involuntarily—even the toes curl up as if clenched like a fist. You are toning your calf, thigh, feet, and toe muscles.

Abdominal Muscles: Besides the firming and toning involuntary muscle contractions that occur within the abdomen, the lifting of the body off the bed during intercourse will also tense and tighten the abdominal muscles. This happens when the pelvis is put into the posture wherein the clitoris presses against the man's pubic bone to achieve maximum pressure and contact.

Pelvic Muscles: The spasmodic contractions of orgasm do much not only to keep the pelvic muscles that surround the vagina and uterus firm, but also to tighten up those muscles in the lower part of the buttocks (those muscles that keep your buttocks from "drooping"). Of course, the longer you prolong these contractions, the firmer these muscles can become.

Cheeks: During the Plateau Phase to orgasm (phase 2) the facial muscles tighten up. This is a *natural* isometric exercise. Proper exercise of these muscles will help fill out furrows that run from the side of the nose to the upper lip. Hollows in the cheek area will also appear more "filled in." Still other facial muscles get a workout, and this helps to give a little lift to cheeks and corners of the mouth.

Mouth Area: Muscles all around the mouth are exercised, and this helps to de-emphasize any nose to mouth furrows, alleviate "pouches" at the corners of the mouth, and in general smooth and firm the skin in this area.

Jaws and Jowls: During orgasm you are exercising the muscle that counteracts the pull of gravity, which creates a flabby jowl area. Also affected are muscles that help prevent a double chin, and the muscle that lessens furrows running from the corners of the mouth to the chin.

Neck: During the buildup stage to orgasm the neck muscles are often being stretched. This, of course, provides exercise to throat muscles, keeping them firm and smooth. (In order for this exercise to be most effective, however, you should make love *without* a pillow under your head, so that the chin will get the ultimate "stretch" out from the neck.)

The Beauty Benefits of Prolonging
Intercourse

Prolonging your lovemaking also prolongs your health and beauty "treatment." For example, it prolongs the period of isometric exercise for your entire body, and the time of increased blood circulation, which is so necessary for the optimum health and maximum beauty of your skin, hair, and nails.

In the Far East and many Moslem countries, techniques for prolonging sexual intercourse have been studied and practiced for centuries. People have always wanted to experience the greatest pleasure for the longest period of time, although it has not been thought of as a "beauty aid" until very recently.

In a pamphlet called "Male Continence," men learned to bring themselves near to their orgasmic threshold, then rest before slowly doing so again, and finally withdraw without ejaculating at all. This technique enabled them to continue sexual inter-course for an hour or so at a time. (These men practiced withdrawal without ejaculation as a method of birth control. But *don't try it* yourself. It's been proven medically unsound, since male semen can be introduced into the vagina in small amounts without ejaculation.)

The most effective method for you to use to prolong an orgasm is by stretching out the pleasurable period preceding it through the process called "teasing." First build up genital tension and learn to maintain it at a peak. (But don't let yourself become stimulated enough to reach orgasm.) Teasing allows for a greater buildup of sexual tension, and the longer you "hold out" with each orgasm, the more beauty benefits you gain.

During this time let yourself go, taking the deep breaths that come naturally through your mouth. Relax and "go with it." Deep breathing causes the heart to beat faster and the flow of blood circulation to speed up. This in turn brings an increase in the oxygen supply throughout the body, which leads to better skin tone. In the process cells are also given a fresh supply of rejuvenating blood, and this encourages all the body's organs to function at a higher peak of efficiency.

Your man will probably love it if you want to prolong your lovemaking. Expressing an interest in doing so is the encouragement he needs. So here are some helpful hints:

1) Both of you read Dr. David Reuben's book, *How to Get More Out of Sex*—together!

2) Spend more time in foreplay. There's no reason to rush things. Extended periods of foreplay not only give intense pleasure, but give you extended "beauty treatments."

3) Talk to him. Tell him what really turns you on. If even you don't know, experiment and find out.

4) Stop every now and then and "wind down." Permit the level of excitement to die down a bit. (This is especially important for the male, who usually reaches the orgasmic state more quickly than the female.) Putting off the orgasmic phase increases the beauty benefits to be derived from lovemaking.

5) If you feel that your partner is coming too close to climax, and still want to prolong the valuable foreplay period, try this simple technique to stop ejaculation: place your hand across his penis with the thumb on the top of the vein running alongside the outside of the penis. Now press hard with the thumb for a moment, then release. This pressure exerted on the vein acts as a tourniquet bandage would; it prevents the seminal fluid from flowing into the glans, thereby preventing ejaculation.

22

How the Proper Vitamins, Minerals, and Nutrition Help You Achieve Beauty-Orgasm

WITHOUT A DOUBT, sex, orgasm, and therefore beauty are directly influenced by the state of your health. In fact, many doctors agree that sexual health and the physical capacity for lovemaking are closely tied to the state of your health generally, your endocrine and sex glands in particular; and nutrition is now thought to be the most important single factor affecting your physical and mental well-being.

Therefore what you eat does have a great bearing on your sexuality and your ability to have orgasms for beauty. This has been borne out scientifically in thousands of tests that show that nutritionally deprived men and women experienced a sharp decline—or even complete disappearance—of sexual drive. Conversely, many people have also reported a marked increase in their sexual drive after dietary improvements were made. In fact, one sixty-year-old widower reported that he felt so much better after beginning a proper diet that he was amazed at his capabilities. However, he felt that he would have to discontinue his new regime, at least until he found a permanent sex partner!

Since by this time I assume that everyone who reads this book is familiar with the foods that make up what is commonly referred to as a "balanced diet," I will confine this chapter to a discussion of some of the special foods that are thought to stimulate your sex glands and improve your orgasms. I'm calling these foods "Orgasm Foods," for they're the foods that act both directly and indirectly in the production of hormones. In addition most of them contribute to the body's basic nutritional needs, which will help to create and maintain a healthy sexual appetite.

Most of the old love potions and lists of aphrodisiac foods one finds in ancient literature read just like a modern textbook on basic nutrition. For instance, here are some of the all-time "favorite" Orgasm Foods, and some more up-to-date findings which prove that the ancients were pretty smart about sex.

Honey Pollen (contained in large amounts in natural, unstrained, and unrefined honey) is probably the active substance in honey responsible for its sexual value. Pollen seems to be the most complete food in nature. It contains 20 percent complete proteins, all the water-soluble vitamins (especially B and C), and plenty of minerals, enzymes, and trace elements.

Pollen is also said to directly stimulate the sex glands because it contains a *gonadotropic hormone,* a plant hormone that is similar to the pituitary hormone gonadotropin, that stimulates the sex glands.

Honey's sugars are in a predigested form, and are quickly absorbed by the bloodstream. Easily obtainable, sugar is vital for many important body functions, including the manufacture of male seminal fluid.

Aspartic acid, said to be the active factor in honey, has been used to treat chronic fatigue, insomnia, and general lethargy in relation to lovemaking—commonly called "bedroom fatigue."

Milk Milk contains all the known vitamins. But for our purposes, perhaps its most important contribution is Vitamin B-12, which is absolutely essential for sexual activity. From a sexual point of view another important component of milk is casein, which is believed to be the highest grade of protein available. This has a material effect on sexuality because sexual activity is stimulated by the hypophyseal hormone, which is produced by the pituitary gland. This hormone is composed of protein, and therefore an adequate intake of protein is required for its continued production. Naturally, the better grade of protein intake, the better grade of this sex-stimulating hormone the body produces.

Sesame Seeds This long-popular seed deserves to be known as an Orgasm Food for quite a few reasons. First, its protein content is 19 percent to 20 percent, which is higher than most red meats. Also, it contains many of the B vitamins, such as niacin, inositol, and choline. This Orgasm Food is richer in calcium than cheese, nuts, or eggs, and is also an excellent source of lecithin and Vitamin E.

Eggs It is in the protein area that eggs score particularly high; the value of their protein is said to be second only to that of milk. In addition, eggs are also a first-rate source of many of the vitamins and minerals required to maintain an active, healthy sex life. They are particularly rich in Vitamin A, all the B vitamins, and Vitamin D. They also contain sexually important minerals such as copper, phosphorus, potassium, and iron. In addition, they have a large amount of lecithin in the yolk; this substance is quite important for the optimum functioning of the sex glands.

Raw Nuts and Seeds (especially pumpkin) These foods are super-rich sources of zinc, which has been scientifically proven to affect the health of the hormone-producing sex glands. They have a high content of phosphorus, which is needed for sugar metabolism, which in turn is vitally linked to the sex drive. In fact, seeds, nuts, and grains are the best food sources of this vital substance.

But the reason nuts, seeds, and grains are reputed to be the most sexually powerful stimulants of all is because they contain the secret of life itself—the germ. In addition, they are a rich natural source of minerals, most of the vitamins (especially B, E, and F), and are an excellent (and cheap) source of proteins.

Just in case my throwing around the names of all these vitamins and minerals has confused you, let me give a few concrete examples to make it absolutely clear to you how valuable these substances are to your sex life and to your orgasms for beauty.

Vitamin A: This vitamin is necessary to maintain optimum health of the membrane tissue throughout the body, but especially the mucous membranes in the female reproductive organs. It may also be beneficial in treating some thyroid gland problems such as goiter.

The B-Complex Vitamins: The B-Complex group is made up of over thirteen different vitamins, several of which are needed before sex hormones can be produced. For example, B-complex vitamins enter into the cellular and tissue construction of the thyroid gland and act as "energizers" to increase the hormonal flow. Vitamin B-12, folic acid, and pantothenic acid (all members of the B-complex family) help relieve mineral exhaustion. Vitamin B-12 is essential for sexual activity and is found in large amounts in the female uterus. B-1 helps the pituitary gland maintain the sex drive at normal level. Choline (still another B vitamin) helps the liver to manufacture hormones. In general, the B-complex vitamins are recommended to ensure against impotence and premature menopause.

Vitamin C: Vitamin C is often recommended to relieve conditions of adrenal exhaustion. One laboratory test proved that when the diet is lacking in this essential vitamin, animals cease breeding activities. However, when proper amounts of this vitamin were added to their diets, normal breeding activities resumed. Also, if a diet is adequate in amounts of Vitamin C, the pituitary gland is saturated with this substance prior to mating, but depleted of it after mating has taken place.

Vitamin E: Vitamin E is often referred to as the "sex vitamin" because it is reputed to restore the sex organs to normalcy, help stimulate the production of sperm, and in general rejuvenate the sex glands. It is needed for normal sex hormone production, and protects these hormones from destruction by oxidation. In addition to this direct effect on the sex glands, Vitamin E has a strong effect on sexual activity through its action on the anterior lobe of the pituitary, which has control over sexual activity. Another example of the indirect effect of Vitamin E is the stimulating effect it has on the thyroid gland. Thyroid hormones are responsible for much of an individual's sex drive. An underactive thyroid gland can cause a person to lose all interest in sexual activity.

Phosphorus: is needed for normal, healthy functioning of the sexual nerve centers. A lack of this essential mineral can result in decreased sexual potency.

Sodium: This substance has been used to treat cases of adrenal exhaustion. Sodium and potassium are also involved in muscle contraction and expansion, and in nerve stimulation.

Potassium: Potassium is considered of special importance for the prevention of various female disorders because of its stimulating influence on endocrine hormone production. (It has been commonly used for treating chronic fatigue and lassitude.)

Zinc: Zinc is essential for the general growth and proper development of the reproductive organs. (It may also be required in the synthesis of DNA, which is the master substance of life, carrying all inherited traits and directing the activity of each cell.) A zinc deficiency can result in delayed sexual maturity, sterility, and in extreme cases, dwarfism.

Personally I have my own special list of Orgasm Foods, some of which I try to include in my diet every day. My choice is based upon their general nutritional value plus their reputed—and in some cases scientifically proven—"aphrodisiac" value. Here they are; I strongly recommend that you try them for yourself:

Apples	Milk or Cream
Asparagus	Nuts
Bananas	Onions
Cucumbers	Oysters
Egg Yolks	Pumpkin Seeds
Figs	Spinach
Garlic	Wheat Germ
Honey	Yogurt

23

Drinking, Smoking, and "the Pill:" Beauty-Orgasm Killers

ASIDE FROM THE very obvious fact that a drunk and sloppy lover is a big turnoff for anyone, the basic properties of alcohol itself make it antisex and as I've already demonstrated, antibeauty. Basically alcohol is a sedative that inhibits and dampens physical and mental reactions. Although it may have a beneficial effect in releasing inhibitions, a continuous use of alcohol, even in small amounts, will eventually bring about a gradual diminution of sexual capacity. In larger amounts, alcohol definitely exerts a paralyzing action on the genitalia.

The following is a quote from the December, 1974, issue of *Prevention* magazine: "Alcohol inhibits the conversion of Vitamin A into a form required for the production of sperm... Simultaneously, the toxic effect of alcohol and the nutritional deficiencies induced by it combine to interfere with breakdown of estrogen (the female hormone) by the liver." What is worse, alcohol acts as a poison on the genital tissues and organs, and can bring about sterility and total atrophy of the reproductive system. Many scientists believe that even before alcohol can cause visible pathological changes and affect the health of the still young and healthy-looking drinker, his potency is all but gone.

The evidence against smoking for those who wish to have a full, healthy sex and beauty life is even stronger. Dr. Magnus Hirschfield believes that the potency of many smoking men and women is adversely affected by their habit. He explains that toxic substances in tobacco have a disturbing effect on the sex-hormone-producing chemistry of the body. Dr. D. W. Hastings, a well-known authority on impotence, reports that when some of his patients stopped smoking, they observed in themselves a markedly increased sexual drive.

Dr. Ilja Porudorninskij reports that nicotine damages the sexual glands and the sexual nerve centers, and that excessive smokers can become impotent as a direct result of smoking. A summary of a 1973 Surgeon General's report, *The Health Consequences of Smoking,* states, "There is strong evidence that smoking mothers have a significantly greater number of unsuccessful pregnancies due to stillbirths and neonatal death."

One of the worst effects of smoking is that it destroys Vitamin C in your body. W. J. McCormock, M. D., the well-known authority on Vitamin C, says that each cigarette destroys about 25 mg.— the equivalent of the vitamin content of one orange. This observation has been confirmed by research in Poland and the United States.

Finally, Dr. Joel Fort, director of San Francisco's Center for Solving Special Social and Health Problems (which helps people to both overcome the cigarette habit and deal with sexual maladjustments), automatically counsels smokers who complain of impotence to enroll in the center's stop-smoking clinic. The overwhelming majority of men who do so, says Dr. Fort, report their sex lives markedly improved. He gives the same advice to women who complain of lack of interest in sex.

Dr. Fort theorizes that smoking impairs sexual performance in two primary ways: the carbon monoxide intake reduces the blood oxygen level and impairs hormone production; the nicotine intake constricts the blood vessels, the swelling of which is the central mechanism of sexual excitement and erection. Dr. Fort also cites secondary effects of heavy smoking: lung capacity is reduced, cutting back on stamina and the ability to "last" during intercourse; nicotine discolors the teeth and taints the breath, reducing the smoker's sexual attractiveness.

Last but not least, any woman who wishes to get the most out of sex, should read this about "the Pill." Although about 10 million women are now using the Pill (approximately one third of all women seeking birth control), there is mounting suspicion that it can cause sexual frigidity and loss of libido in some women. Although two out of three female doctors will recommend the Pill to her patients, only one out of three is using it herself!

Dr. William Masters (the Masters of Masters and Johnson) counsels patients who are referred to him for treatment of frigidity to stop using oral contraceptives for a period of six months. He finds that in most instances the problem clears up during this time and no other measures are necessary.

Dr. J. E. Eichenlaub, a Minneapolis gynecologist, told a marriage seminar in Kansas City, Missouri, that about 20 percent of women feel a stronger sexual interest toward the end of their menstrual period, when there is a lower progesterone circulation in the system. When progesterone circulation is at its height, as during pregnancy or the beginning of the menstrual period, they show a virtually complete disinterest in sex. The pill spreads progesterone action through the system during the entire month, and plays havoc with a woman's sexual responsiveness.

Although the "soft drugs"—mainly marijuana and hashish—have been touted by many lately as "aphrodisiac" because of their inhibition-lessening effect, I strongly urge against their use. Before you label me as an "old fogey" and hopelessly "square," I'd like to explain why.

While they may make you feel more sexual for the moment, like alcohol they tend to have an adverse long-range effect in which the sex drive is gradually lessened and finally disappears altogether. Also, like alcohol, habitual users tend to neglect their dietary requirements, leading to an overall diminution of health and, naturally, sexual ability.

Frankly, I would even caution against the use of coffee after a meal, before an evening of lovemaking. Coffee acts as an antirelaxant, and the overstimulation of the caffeine might sabotage your amorous intentions. If you're in the right frame of mind, and with the person you love, your partner will be "intoxicating" enough!

24

The Problem of "Frigidity"

OBVIOUSLY, IF YOU aren't having orgasms, you can't reap the benefits I've been discussing. You might now be pretending to reach an orgasm because you believe this is necessary to your partner's pleasure and ego-enhancement. You might believe that if you don't act as if you're responding, you will not seem sexually adequate or attractive to your man.

If this is the way it is for you, you may believe yourself to be hopelessly frigid. However, I'd like to make it clear that a woman who does not experience orgasms should not be automatically labeled "frigid" by anyone, including *herself*. Frigidity means coldness, a distaste for sex; a nonorgasmic woman, however, usually needs and enjoys sex but cannot reach a climax or, if she does, it happens rarely. She is far more common than the frigid woman, and is often mistaken for her.

Although it is possible for a woman to have a satisfactory marriage with a tolerable sex life, and never or very infrequently attain orgasm, all normal women should regularly achieve orgasm, and if they don't there's always a sound, *un*-natural reason. So if you're not experiencing orgasm, you must do something about it. A woman's body is built for pleasure—in fact, the clitoris has ten times more sexual nerve endings packed into it than the penis. Therefore you should have the ability to experience ten times more sexual pleasure than your man!

Authorities such as Havelock Ellis and Sigmund Freud, and more recently, Dr. Alfred Kinsey, Dr. Mary Jane Sherfey, and Masters and Johnson have all confirmed the fact that the female—unlike the male—can experience several orgasms in rapid succession during intercourse. A recent issue of *Prevention* magazine reported that a study made by Dr. L. M. Terman in 1938 showed that of some 800 women investigated, 13 percent experienced multiple orgasms. Dr. Kinsey, from a roughly similar sample, reported 14 percent. Masters' and Johnson's research also confirmed these findings. They stated categorically, "If a female who is capable of having a regular orgasm is properly stimulated within a short time after her first climax, she will, in most instances, be capable of having a second, third, fourth, even fifth orgasm..."

Dr. Sherfey, a student of Dr. Kinsey, and an outstanding psychiatrist in her own right, published a paper in the *Journal of the American Psychoanalytic Association* in which she stated, "The more orgasms a woman has, the stronger they become. The more orgasms she has, the more she can have." Dr. Sherfey's conclusion is summed up in one sentence: "The human female is in fact not sexually inadequate or inferior, *if freed from cultural restrictions..."*

Therefore simply having the right information about sex and their own bodily response to it would "de-frigid" thousands of women. In most cases where a woman is called (or thinks of herself as) "frigid," the problem really stems from "old wives' tales" and ignorance (sometimes compounded by fear) on the part of the woman herself, and/or her partner.

Once again—if you're not experiencing orgasm, you owe it to yourself and your partner to do something about it! Stop suffering... stop telling yourself that it's not important for you to enjoy sex. Sex is a vital and perfectly natural and important part of any adult's life, male or female. God built our bodies as they are—as vehicles for our pleasure and that of our lover. If you feel that you're not experiencing the pleasure that is your health and beauty right, go over these checkpoints to see if any one of them could help you to achieve your full sexual potential.

1) If you've been pretending to have an orgasm for a long period of time, it may be difficult to now tell this to your husband. But you could say something like, "I'm no longer having an orgasm— let's try something new." Or visit your family doctor and ask his advice on what to do. He should be able to help. Don't feel embarrassed about this. According to doctors, there are *many* women who don't experience orgasm, and it's been often proven to be due to lack of the proper information on the man's part.

2) It is assumed that by the time she marries, a

woman is reasonably knowledgeable about sex (even though she may be a virgin), and mentally free of the psychological restrictions that may have been placed upon sex during her childhood and young adulthood. In fact, this is not always the case. For after years of being warned to repress her natural sexual urges, a woman may find it difficult to really "open up" to her husband when the wedding night finally arrives. After all, placing a gold band on the third finger of her left hand is not all it takes to turn a girl, who has been taught (under pain of sin or punishment) to carefully guard her "virtue," into a highly responsive, sensual, sexually mature woman. Even if the desire to be so is there, she may have gotten so conditioned to stopping at a certain point during the prelude to lovemaking that she now is automatically short-circuiting her own pleasure mechanism.

If this description might apply in your case, my first advice to you is to read everything about sex you can get your hands on. In this way you will condition your mind to what is normal and natural about sex, and perhaps "psych" yourself out of all those old taboos and restrictions. It also might be helpful if you would read this material over with your partner. Then together you may be able to explore some new, more exciting sexual variations. In any case, let him know that you really want to "grow up" sexually, and that you're willing to experiment. I'm sure that if you just ask for his help, he'll be more than willing to give it.

3) A primary cause of female sexual inadequacy is dyspareunia, or pain during the sex act. This pain may have a real, physical origin, or it may

originate in the mind. Mild pain is actually the worst, for severe pain will call attention to itself until a visit to the doctor is made. But mild pain, vaguely felt, is often ignored. Yet if it is allowed to continue for any length of time, it may really turn a woman off to the idea of intercourse.

Lack of vaginal lubrication is one basic cause of pain during intercourse. Although it is necessary and usually present, lubrication can be blocked by various factors, for example: fear of pregnancy or of disease, fear of pain itself, guilt over the act itself, or lack of estrogenic hormones—a condition common to women during the menopause or after.

If you are around the age of menopause (roughly forty-five to fifty-five) and find yourself experiencing less and less sexual gratification, it may be due to the lessening of these very important hormones. First see your doctor, and tell him that intercourse is painful, and that you feel "dry" during lovemaking. (This won't be a new complaint for him—he's heard it many times before.) He will then probably prescribe replacement hormones. This treatment should enable you to regain the vaginal fluids you had as a young woman.

If you find that a visit to the doctor is impractical—or simply impossible—at this time, you may substitute vaginal lubrication for your own natural fluids. A bland vaginal cream (such as K-Y jelly, or even Vaseline) can be purchased in drug stores, and simply inserted into the vagina before intercourse.

4) Dr. Helen Singer Kaplan, clinical associate professor of psychiatry at Cornell University School of Medicine and author of *The New Sex*

Therapy (Quadrangle, 1974), says that lack of sexual interest can reflect underlying debilitating illness, fatigue, worry, depression, and the use and abuse of certain drugs. Fluctuating hormonal states (as during the menstrual cycle or pregnancy) also have a direct bearing upon your sexual arousal level. The use of contraceptive medicine can also change this hormonal level; many women lose some interest in sex when they take "the Pill."

5) If you've checked out all of the above possibilities and find that they definitely don't apply to you, and yet you still derive no satisfaction from lovemaking, this might be the answer.

Frequently during childbirth (or multiple childbirths), or after the menopause, the vaginal tissues lose their elasticity, and thus the pleasurable sensations during intercourse are lessened—or sometimes disappear completely. In this case, a simple surgical procedure known as an "anterior posterior repair" might be the answer. It is performed for no other reason than to heighten female sexual satisfaction, and it is designed to increase penis-vagina friction during sex, and thus the pleasure *and* beauty that follows.

The whole procedure takes less than an hour, and it can make a mother of five (or grandmother of fifty-five) almost "virginally tight." What takes place is this: during the operation, the excess vaginal tissue is pulled together, muscles and supportive tissues are reinforced, and bladder and uretha restored to their correct position. If you're interested, ask your gynecologist more about it.

Are You Inhibiting Your Own Beauty-Orgasms?

Many women say that they do not have a fulfilling sex life—and most of them blame it on their husbands. But before we do this too quickly, let's go through this simple checklist to see if at least *part* of the blame shouldn't be ours.

1) Do you always leave the total responsibility for initiating lovemaking to your husband?

2) Do you make him "take" your body instead of giving it freely and joyously?

3) Do you know what turns your husband on?

4) Did you ever try to find out?

5) Do you ever ask your husband if he is totally pleased with you sexually?

6) Are you predictable in bed? Is your lovemaking always the same?

7) Does your bedroom look relaxing and inviting?

8) Are you keeping up with the new sexual studies such as those by Masters and Johnson and Dr. David Reuben? Do you read books and articles on the subject of obtaining sexual satisfaction?

9) Do you go to bed with curlers in your hair? With all the home hair dryers on the market today, in all price ranges, this is really unnecessary. However, if for some good reason you must go to bed in curlers, at least cover them completely with a fresh, pretty scarf.

10) Do you sleep in a garment you would never have dreamed of wearing when you were first married?

11) Do you know how to use sexual fantasies constructively in your sexual relationship?

12) Do you ever wear oily night creams to bed when you make love? This is a real turnoff for most men. Of course, you should wear a night cream or moisturizer while you sleep, but put the jar on the nightstand, and apply it *after* lovemaking.

13) Do you let him see that he excites you sexually? Don't hold back. Knowing how he turns *you* on is very exciting to him.

14) Are you warm and affectionate during the day as well as at night? This builds up his confidence, making him a better lover when the time comes.

15) Do *you* ever woo *him?* Leave a sexy note in his lunch pail or briefcase... or mail it to him at home or his office. Buy him a "surprise" present once in a while.

16) Are you willing to make love at "unorthodox" times?

If you cannot answer at least fourteen of these questions positively, you have some homework to do *before* you even approach him.

25

The "Complete" Woman

"I'M GLAD I'M FORTY," said Sophia Loren. "I wouldn't be any other age. I have never felt better about myself. Forty is my most joyous birthday because I have finally found myself; know who I am and what I need. I have never felt younger, because I am finally fulfilled." In short, she's a Complete Woman.

Contrast that joy of living with the statement of Princess Grace of Monaco upon reaching her fortieth birthday: "I think turning forty is miserable. It's something you know is going to happen, but you think, why so soon? Forty is a marvelous age for a man, but for a woman it is torture, the end."

I wonder if Princess Grace ever sat and chatted with Jean-Baptiste Troisgros, bon vivant and guiding spirit of one of France's most celebrated restaurants. I doubt it, for if she had she would have faced forty with a smile on her face instead of a frown. M. Troisgros passed away recently at the age of seventy-seven, but during his lifetime he held forth on everything from food to sex and politics; and he was widely quoted. On women: "At forty-five the devil takes over, and they're beautiful, splendid, maternal, proud. The acidities are gone, and in their place reigns calm. They are worth going out to find and, because of them, some men never grow old. When I see them, my mouth waters."

I hope Princess Grace has changed her mind about age. Or soon that negative attitude will write itself across her lovely face for everyone to see. Hers is very definitely not the 29 Forever attitude, which has no room for regret. To quote Sophia Loren again, "Regret only makes wrinkles." Gloria Vanderbilt, who is in her early fifties, looks years younger, and whose career as a painter and designer gets more fabulous every year, says, "If your 'inside' life—the *human* side—is right, then the outside things will be right, too." She's correct, of course. The 29 Forever woman is a Complete Woman—a blend of charming outer appearance and inner worth. She feels happy, content, freer inside . . . so she looks beautiful outside.

The 29 Forever woman doesn't worry about age. She knows that if you really care for people beyond yourself you remain young and forever desirable. A life free from selfishness is the secret of Eternal Youth. Age holds no terror for her.

Nor for her male counterpart, either. On the occasion of his most recent birthday, the great French film director Jean Renoir looked out at the world and exclaimed, "The adventure of being eighty years old is that one has had so many people to love." *Bravo!*

Age, you see, is how you feel about yourself. To

quote Cary Grant, who knows a thing about staying youthful, "Enjoy yourself, which means just that—enjoy being *you.*"

You can't fake how you feel about *you.* Your clothes, your makeup, your hairdo, your diet, your perfume, your posture, your voice—everything about you—advertises how you feel about *you.*

Certainly, before you can love another, you have to love yourself enough. That's why Sophia Loren, past forty, is 29 Forever; and so is her mother. "She is still a great beauty, inside and out," says Sophia. "She gives instead of taking, which is the secret ingredient of remaining young. She accepts all that comes with life and welcomes each new state. She takes care of everybody, and she takes care of herself, mentally, spiritually, physically."

All 29 Forever women have that in common. Gloria Swanson has more drive and energy than many women half her age. This past year this stunning-looking great-grandmother married a man some fifteen years her junior. Glorious Gloria is also vitally interested in nutrition and simply can't grant an interview without talking about it. "The public has always been good to me," she explains, "and I feel that I ought to pass along what I know about it and what I believe in."

Actress Merle Oberon, one of the great beauties of our time, who looks at least twenty years younger than her calendar years, and now wed to a handsome man many years younger than she, says, "You know, it shocks me when people tell me how young I look, because inside I feel exactly as I did twenty or thirty years ago! It's terribly important to 'think' young. Many women just give up at forty or fifty, and then they tend to get bitter or sour. One should also *think* kind . . . envy and greed take a toll on looks."

Arlene Dahl of the red hair, green eyes, and pearlized complexion became a mother again at age forty-five. She believes "The great beauty secret in the world is love . . . it gives enormous fringe benefits. When you're in love and being loved, your whole body works better!"

Why in the world should any woman allow her chronological age to discourage her from expecting love? From now on, women will stay younger longer, because they know so much more about taking care of themselves—good diet, good exercise. So-called "middle age" is moving up to sixty! Love nourishes you and keeps you young. *Indulge*.

"Love is extremely useful to women in terms of health, beauty, and youth—it makes them bloom," says Dr. Ivan Popov, the celebrated European youth doctor. "Women," he maintains, "definitely have a greater sexual capacity than men, and sex is much better in every way for them."

I have always found older men more attractive than younger men. Many a mature woman begins to find younger men increasingly attractive; and many an under-thirty man finds an older, more sophisticated woman a fantastic lover and companion. So I make no romantic predictions for myself; in fact, no predictions at all, other than that I plan to go through life enjoying each moment to the fullest. I am determined not to permit my mind to get rigid—about fashion, morals, love, *anything*.

Nor should you. Never allow yourself to get so smug and comfortable that you resist change.

Instead seek it out. Develop the habit of curiosity, the habit of people...the habit of laughter. It will keep your mind and spirit young and elastic—alive with anticipation.

A cosmetically beautiful woman may be stared at the most, but it's the woman who enjoys herself the most who winds up with a cluster of admirers around her!

Always try the new and different...a *new* food...a *new* perfume...a *new* hobby...a *new* language...a *new* friend...a *new* lover. Sometimes just a *new* way to reach a familiar destination. The very act of trying will energize your personality and take you deeper and deeper into a love affair with Life.

Then you will be *29 FOREVER!*

BERKLEY BESTSELLERS YOU WON'T WANT TO MISS!